# AN UNFADING VISION

# VISION

*The adventure of books*

CW00538618

Edward England

## HODDER AND STOUGHTON

LONDON   SYDNEY   AUCKLAND   TORONTO

**British Library C.I.P.**

England, Edward
   An unfading vision: the adventure of books.
  1. Hodder and Stoughton Limited—History
  2. Christian literature—Publication and
  distribution—Great Britain
  I. Title
  338.7'610705'0941      Z325

  ISBN 0 340 27603 7

To ANN with love

# CONTENTS

# 1

# THE ADVENTURE

'At any moment an unsatisfying life may become once more a grand adventure if we will surrender it to God,' wrote Dr. Paul Tournier, the Swiss psychiatrist. I believed him and my life was changed. Within weeks of reading those words I was launched on a new career: discovering the adventure of books; the adventure of authors; the adventure of God.

Books have influenced my life as enduringly as family, friends, church or environment. Is that an exaggeration? I think not. About every ten years my direction has been radically altered by a book. It was *The Adventure of Living*, by Paul Tournier, that brought me into publishing.

In 1966 as a London bookseller I received an advance copy which I slipped into my briefcase to read on the train. Going home the evening newspaper occupied the journey, but next morning I took the book out as the train left Purley, a leafy suburb fourteen miles from London.

Dr. Tournier practised medicine in Geneva but I was aware of his international reputation that depended little on drugs or surgery. His large-format paperback had three divisions: 'The Adventure', 'The Risk' and 'The Choice'. As I opened it I had no premonition that when I closed the book at Victoria Station, twenty-five minutes away, I would have been jolted into a decision which would affect the rest of my life.

For nine years I had been the manager of a religious bookshop in London's West End. I expected to remain a bookseller, but my position had ceased to be an adventure, initiative had died. Day by day I carried on, comfortable, surrounded by congenial company and plentiful reading. In twenty-nine years I would receive a pension. My first years had been creative but a mechanical routine had settled in.

Make no mistake, a bookseller is favoured. He can discover for himself, as Sir Francis Bacon suggested, which books are to be tasted, which are to be swallowed and the few which are to be chewed and digested. Yet, through Tournier, as in a mirror, I saw myself reposing in a rut; a rut which was becoming a grave. I had mastered the detail, was no longer being stretched or fulfilled, was able to depend too readily on an excellent staff. It would have been a challenge if some destructive force had threatened us, if for economic reasons the bookshop had been faced with closure, or if the twenty-two assistants had gone on strike.

Dr. Tournier talked of the adventure of God being worked out in every human adventure. 'The Bible is the book of adventure and must be read as such. Not only the adventure of the world and of humanity, but the personal adventure of each man and woman whom God touches, calls, and sends into action.'

I turned the pages. 'The God of the Bible is the God who acts,' I read. 'This is what distinguishes him from the God of the philosophers and from the gods of all the other religions. He is the God who commits himself in every man's life. He does not interest himself only in man's religious life but in his whole life, in his work, in his occupation – as potter, as shepherd, as official, as house-wife – and he turns that occupation into a veritable adventure.'

The train stopped momentarily at Croydon and Clapham Junction. I barely noticed. Was there a new adventure for me? To be in a rut at thirty-five was lamentable. I might step out and fail, but all adventure carried that risk. The other passengers were stretching to the luggage racks for their briefcases and coats to begin the final stage of the office trek.

'The answer lies in the surrender of our lives to God, for he is the very source of life, a source that is always new. He brings one adventure to an end only to open another to us. He is tireless and inexhaustible. With him we must be ready for anything.'

To live is to choose. C. S. Lewis said: 'Every time you make a choice you are turning the central part of you, the part of you that chooses, into something a little different from what it was before.'

What were those Old Testament words? 'I have set before you life and death . . . therefore choose life' (Deut. 30:19).

What about the bookshop's need? If I left to embark on my own adventure would it suffer? No. To pretend I was irreplaceable was nonsense, a defensive shield. For my successor the bookshop would be an adventure.

Was I hearing the voice of God, or responding to my own restlessness? It was easier to ask the question than to know the answer, but as the train lost its passengers at Victoria Station I told myself that a West End bookshop was about to lose its manager. I believed God had spoken.

I had no indication of the place or nature of my future, at home or abroad, in the world of books or some other sphere, but I believed by leaving the bookshop I would be setting out on a road of growth, surrendering an unsatisfying life. No orator, no music, no friend, could have produced a more fervent response than my reading of *The Adventure of Living*.

I quickly paced the one and a half miles from Victoria to the bookshop; past Buckingham Palace, with its handful of sightseers and cameras, across Green Park clothed in the freshness of spring, up exclusive Bond Street.

Choosing means renouncing. I was fortunate: I could leave the buying and selling of books with a quiet conscience. For others the choice might mean remaining where they were, whatever the drabness, monotony, pain, hardship. For them to leave might be irresponsible.

I sat at my book-littered desk, overlooking the top of the medical profession's Harley Street, conscious that we had recently doubled the frontage of this Scripture Union bookshop, taking over an opticians and a health-food store, that we had become chartered booksellers. Scripture Union was evangelical, esteemed worldwide for its ministry among children and young people and its graded Bible reading aids. Alongside its old public school image was a growing concern for the less privileged. Its General Secretary, Dr. John Laird, with a global view, directed with statesmanlike qualities.

Our well-heeled customers – professional men, slender business girls, elegant West End shoppers – were concerned with what they purchased and with what we stocked. Some protested that our windows should permanently display the publications of the newly-founded Banner of Truth Trust, largely reprints of solid works by the Puritans; others read only titles from the Inter-Varsity Press. We stocked all the books from both but were wary of the S.C.M. Press with its more liberal tradition. I had been compelled to read *The Adventure of Living* before placing an order because it came from S.C.M.

Books by non-evangelicals were rarely stocked, never without a thorough vetting. In the buying of stock I had been given remarkable freedom within Scripture Union's biblical perspective, but I had occasionally been overruled, sometimes shatteringly, as in the case of two books by C. S. Lewis. The former Professor of Medieval and Renaissance English Literature at Cambridge, who had earlier taught English literature and language at Oxford, would not have worried. His concern as a writer was not to be accepted, but to express himself honestly. 'When you have done so, the rest lies with God,' he wrote. His classic *The Problem of Pain* had been judged unsuitable. When *The Four Loves* was published it was declared unsound. Yet he succeeded, as few others, in presenting 'that which is timeless (the same yesterday, today, and tomorrow) in the particular language of our own age.'

In the bookshop we promoted Dr. J. B. Phillips' translation of the New Testament, but his book *The Four Prophets* had to be removed from the window when a customer complained that the jacket mentioned *two* Isaiahs.

The first charismatic title by the Reverend Michael Harper, a curate of All Souls', Langham Place, five minutes away from the bookshop, disappeared from the shelves following an appraisal by a Scripture Union editor, but the author remained a loyal customer, indeed one of our best. He liked the company of C. S. Lewis and J. B. Phillips.

Although these border-line books, and fifty or so like them, were banned from exhibition on the shelves we kept them discreetly in the 'black cupboard' for mature customers. An unmarked hideaway, it included William Barclay's *Daily Study Bible* and paperbacks for adolescent girls and newly-married couples.

'Any new heresies?' those in the know would ask. What was hidden was desirable.

Although the bookshop today maintains its strong evangelical position, its stocking policy has been somewhat relaxed. C. S. Lewis, J. B. Phillips and Michael Harper have been unveiled and given prominence with authors like Martyn Lloyd-Jones, John R. W. Stott, and J. I. Packer. Mothers no longer have to ask for books for growing girls. Paul Tournier has a regular slot.

I left my office and strolled over to Scripture Union's bustling administrative headquarters in Marylebone Lane. There was a sense of adventure. I was about to burn my boats. 'The adventure of faith,' said Tournier, 'is exciting, difficult, and exacting, but full of poetry, of new discoveries, of fresh turns and sudden surprises.'

As I entered the door and ran up the stairs to the first floor I knew I was going to miss this honoured society, with its high standards, its edifying range of Christian activity, serving the local church, never in competition with it. The business manager gave a cheery greeting as I entered his office. More than most busy men he had time for callers.

'I've read *The Adventure of Living*, a new book by Paul Tournier,' I told him. 'It's made me think. Hard. I'm in a rut and the rut is becoming a grave. I've decided to leave the bookshop and make a new start.'

'It's a bit sudden,' he said soberly, without reproach. 'Are you sure?'

'Yes. I love the bookshop. And my colleagues. And some of the customers. Frankly, I owe S.U. a big, big debt. But it holds the last nine years – not my future. I must look forward not back.'

I had not told Gwen. She disliked change. The thought troubled me as I travelled home that evening. I should have telephoned and talked it over, left the options open, not told the business manager until we had discussed it. That, at least, was demanded in a marriage partnership. How would she react? The possibility of my changing jobs had not arisen in recent conversation. Our talk had been of swopping the car.

She was preparing the evening meal in the kitchen as I walked up from the garage and climbed the steps to the back door. It was a snug bungalow with a big view across the green valley. When I first saw that view, and the two hundred rose bushes in the garden, I decided I wanted to purchase the property but happily Gwen shared that decision with me. I opened the kitchen door, filled with apprehension, rehearsing the words.

'I'm leaving the bookshop, dear. I told Charles today.'

'You what?'

'I'm going to give up my job and make a fresh start.'

She put down the vegetables. There was a long moment of silence, then the questions tumbled out. I put my arm around her. 'It's going to be all right.'

'Why didn't you say at breakfast?'

'I didn't know.'

'You must have been thinking about it.'

'Not until I read the book. I thought I was content as a bookseller, then I saw I wasn't. Not deep down. Not for ever. It's a matter of choice. Opting for security, or stepping into the unknown. All change inevitably involves risk.'

She turned to the stove. 'And you don't have anywhere to go?'

'I'd wondered about publishing.'

I wrote to two publishers. My background in provincial journalism, my years as manager of a specialist bookshop, made publishing appear a good idea. I started by applying at the top: to Hodder and Stoughton and to William Collins, both general publishers with flourishing religious lists, both of whom were at ease with C. S. Lewis and J. B. Phillips. Three days later I received a telephone call from Leonard Cutts, a senior director of Hodder and Stoughton. Would it be convenient for me to call at their offices, St. Paul's House, Warwick Lane, that afternoon? The chairman would like to see me.

There was no space to prepare for an interview. I travelled by underground train from the West End to the City recalling the little I had learned about Hodders. Their London representative, John McGinty, called weekly: he was among the best. Their books were on my shelves at home, and in the bookshop. I did not know they had been served by only three religious editors in ninety-nine years of publishing; that Leonard Cutts had started his distinguished career in that role nearly thirty-five years before.

A small, perfectly-tailored man in his sixties, he greeted me with old-fashioned courtesy, taking my coat and putting it on the hat stand with his black bowler before sitting at the antique dining-table which substituted for an executive desk. He had an ecclesiastical bearing, a hint of a time gone by. After relaxed conversation he took me to meet Robin Denniston, the editorial director, whose rolled-up sleeves and demeanour suggested he did not wear a bowler, and then to Paul Hodder-Williams, the chairman.

He explained that Leonard Cutts would be retiring soon. If I had written in any of the three previous decades my chances of an entry into religious publishing at Hodders would have been negligible, but now Hodders wished to make an appointment in preparation for Mr. Cutts' retirement. My letter had been propitiously timed.

'There is a vacancy. When can you start?' he asked.

Had I misheard? He was offering me an opening! I left the prestigious offices jubilant. Publishing was to be my adventure.

'Gwen,' I shouted down the telephone, 'I'm going to be an editor at Hodders.'

'Buy a new suit,' she said.

I was staying in the book world and with Christian books. I believed in them. That belief had been strengthened a few months earlier when I had attended a lecture given by Dr. William Barclay.

'A book,' he said, 'can be a dynamic and explosive power for good or for evil, and, once it is printed and sold, nothing can stop the dissemination of its ideas. We are in a situation in which there is laid upon author, publisher and bookseller an unparalleled responsibility for the dissemination and communication of Christian truth, and it may not be an exaggeration to say that the future of the Christian faith depends on how we together face that responsibility.'

I came to believe my reading of *The Adventure of Living*

had been providential, that Tournier was correct: God was concerned with a man's work, his occupation – as potter, as shepherd, as official, as housewife, as publisher.

'Do not the words sound arrogant, as if we presumed to claim to be favourites of God?' wrote Dr. W. R. Matthews, once Dean of St. Paul's Cathedral, in his autobiography. 'Yet some turning points are so decisive and open up such unforeseen opportunities that we do feel bound to take them as due to the grace of God.'

# 2

# THE DIALOGUE

Hodder and Stoughton came into existence in 1868 as a partnership between two laymen, Matthew Hodder and T. W. Stoughton, who, as part of their evangelism, wanted to publish books which would spread the Gospel.

The founding partners were from Bible-based Puritan stock. The first five books announced in the *Publisher's Circular* of July 1st, 1868, included three Biblical titles: *Jesus Christ, His Times Life and Work*; *Christianity and Modern Progress* and *The Origin of the Four Gospels*. The commitment to religious books had not lapsed. An account of the company issued shortly after my arrival, referring to the desire of the founders to proclaim the Gospel, stated: 'For many years that was the sole purpose of the firm and it is still, after a hundred years, a very vital part of our activities.'

The years immediately after 1918 saw the phenomenal expansion of the fiction and general publishing lists, followed by the Teach Yourself series, and educational and children's books, to make a broad-based enterprise. During these years Sir Ernest Hodder-Williams with Cecil Stoughton, and later Percy Hodder-Williams, all descendants of the founders, directed the company.

The name William Robertson Nicoll had long been known to me. He was probably the most versatile and respected editor ever on the Hodder staff. The firm's association with him began in 1884 when he agreed to edit the *Expositor*. Two years later he persuaded the partners to found a weekly religious newspaper, the *British Weekly*, and from that same year he also acted as Hodder's literary advisor. His biographer, T. H. Darlow, says: 'Side by side with his devotion to literature, Nicoll had another passion, even more dominating and controlling. His supreme interest lay in Christian theology as attested by Christian experience. At the bottom of his soul this accomplished man of literature always remained a sincere and humble believer.'

He was brought up in the Free Church manse at Lumsden, a bleak, lonely village of five or six hundred people, near Aberdeen. His father, the Reverend Harry Nicoll, was a bookworm. The ruling passion of his life was to read and collect books: his income never quite reached £200 a year and was often nearer £100, yet before he died he had accumulated 17,000 volumes – the largest private library of any minister in Scotland. His son told how, for example, he possessed about a hundred editions of the Greek New Testament. If life was frugal there were compensations in the library.

In 1872, Nicoll, then twenty-one, was 'licensed to preach', and on May 12th, he delivered his first sermon. His ordination took place in 1874. His father gave an impressive address: 'He has been three and twenty years with me and I am not tired of him yet, and I hope he will be three and twenty years with you and that you will not be tired of him.' The hope was not fulfilled. Three years later his first book, *Calls to Christ*, was published, giving him an urge for a life of writing and publishing.

His own reading was as prodigious in quantity as his father's had been. He read Boswell's *Johnson* at least twenty times, Lockhart's *Scott* six times and *Rob Roy* sixty times.

Seeing a list of the books he wrote, planned, compiled and edited for Hodder it is puzzling to know how he had any moments at all for relaxed reading but he was a man of ability who, as a friend declared, 'could and did live in half a dozen worlds at once'.

Hodder and Stoughton gave him an opportunity to use his initiative and energy and they were rewarded by tireless industry. In 1909 he received a knighthood; he died in 1923.

There could not have been a better age for him. His father was not alone in putting books on the shelves before

18

beef on the table. In every library then, there were representative selections on religion and theology.

By June 1966, when I entered publishing, the market for these books had dwindled. What manse could boast of 17,000 volumes? Clergy, it was said, now read reviews instead of books.

For nearly a century Hodder and Stoughton's London home had been within sight of St. Paul's Cathedral. From the end of the sixteenth century publishers had been located in the neighbourhood, but Paternoster Row, home of numerous publishers, was demolished by bombs in 1940 and the Hodder building received a direct hit. A reporter who picked his way gingerly from brick to brick recognised nothing but a pillar box, the top beneath his feet. The Publishers' Association estimated that in the first eighteen months of the war more than twenty million volumes were destroyed. Some companies, like Hodder, re-built on the site, others moved away from the Cathedral.

St. Paul's, designed by Wren, is the third Christian church to be built at the top of Ludgate Hill. In 1087 it was almost completely destroyed by fire. Its replacement, known as Old St. Paul's, was completed in the middle of the thirteenth century. This was destroyed in the Great Fire of London in 1666. The new St. Paul's was finished forty-six years after the Great Fire.

I marvelled that the Cathedral still stood. From August 1940 to March 1945, London had known heavy damage from high-explosive bombs, incendaries, flying-bombs and rockets, but although showered by incendaries and damaged by high explosives in October 1940 and April 1941, it miraculously escaped irreparable damage. The blast of the second direct hit lifted the dome but it settled back again in its original situation.

'If one wanted to use the word "miracle" in connection with the preservation of St. Paul's,' said the Dean, 'I would suggest this is the point.'

St. Paul's had exercised a beneficial influence over Hodder, and indeed over the whole city of London, and it was to do the same for me. Being forty-five minutes early on my first day, I went into the Cathedral to pray. It was chilly with a few dim lights casting shadows.

19

St. Paul's speaks to me of God and of the crafts and skills he has given to men down the centuries. It has a timelessness which suggests the eternal, an unhurried God. Within walls heavy with history I sought him. As I knelt down I felt inadequate. I was. How could I make a contribution in this creative world of literature?

My bookshop colleagues, knowing my ignorance, as part of my farewell had given me a copy of Philip Unwin's *Book Publishing as a Career*. I had read of the art, the craft, and the business aspects. The *art* of the publisher is his ability to find and attract authors, often to feed them with ideas, and to have enough of their books to build up and sustain a business. His *craft* enables him to fashion the author's manuscript into suitably designed, well-printed books. His *business* sense keeps it all solvent. I had some business sense and I might develop the art, but I had no knowledge at all of the craft of making manuscripts into beautiful books.

I was stepping into a world of professionals. My consolation was the realisation that Hodder was so diversified, so well-established, so professional, that I could probably do little harm.

Had Matthew Hodder and T. W. Stoughton also knelt here to pray? They were not Anglicans, but the business had started outside the massive doors, and both men prayed. I groped for words and recalled the request of the boy Samuel in the Temple: 'Speak, Lord, for your servant hears.'

And God spoke. As clearly, as distinctly as a voice from the pulpit. It was not an audible voice. It was a revelation, a glimpse of my smallness and of God's greatness, of my restricted outlook and the breadth of his purpose; of his Spirit gently moving through the whole Christian church, bringing men to himself.

*'Do not limit your Christian publishing by your own experience. Publish for the whole church of Jesus Christ. For all men who truly believe that Jesus is the Son of God.'*

'For the Archbishop of Canterbury?'

'If he believes.'

'For the Salvation Army, Lord?'

'They are part of the Body of Christ.'
'For charismatics?'
'Yes.'
'For Billy Graham, Lord?'
'For Billy Graham.'
'And C. S. Lewis?'
'Yes.'
'But not for . . . ?'
'For *all* who know Jesus Christ as Lord.'

There was to be no denominational limit or barrier. Within every arm of the church there were believers, and in every one apostates. I was to seek out the believers.

It was afterwards, when I meditated on the revelation of that morning which hinged around the Lordship of Jesus Christ, that I saw how apt it was that it should have been given in a Cathedral named after St. Paul. His writings were haunted by the word Lord. It was the name he repeatedly used for Jesus. For him Jesus was Lord. Once he had believed himself to be responsible for his own destiny: on the Damascus Road he became a conscript of Christ.

The first words he used on his conversion were, 'Who art thou, Lord?' From that moment he regarded himself as Christ's. In every letter, in every sermon, in every decision he acknowledged his Lordship.

Because I was listening for God I heard. Because I heard I was aware I was not alone as I began a new career. There was a sense of the holy. There would be no distinction between work and prayer. My daily life would be a prayer, listening and responding to God. My anxiety vanished.

I was to publish for all who knew Jesus Christ as Lord. For men whose lives were controlled by Jesus, who, in the words of the Apostle, had presented their bodies a living sacrifice, holy, acceptable to God, men who were living not according to the tradition of men, according to the elements of this world, but 'according to Christ'.

'Woe is unto me, if I preach not the Gospel,' Paul said. 'I am an envoy of Christ,' he told the Corinthians. Knowing I would fail miserably at times, that the light of faith might dim, I nevertheless quietly vowed that morning that I

21

would be a publisher for Christ. I was beginning a mission and this was my 'ordination'.

In an ordination service the bishop asks: 'Are you persuaded that the Holy Scriptures contain sufficiently all doctrine required of necessity for eternal salvation through faith in Jesus Christ? And are you determined, out of the said Scriptures to instruct the people committed to your charge, and to teach nothing, as required of necessity to eternal salvation, but that which you shall be persuaded may be concluded and proved by the Scriptures?'

When the answer has been given, 'I am so persuaded, and have so determined by God's grace,' the bishop goes on to another question. 'Will you be ready, with all faithful diligence, to banish and drive away all erroneous and strange doctrine contrary to God's word?' and the answer must be, 'I will, the Lord being my helper.'

The ceremony takes place with music, colourful robes, and the pomp and ceremony of the Anglican communion. No one was present to lay hands on my head, there was no witness, but I look back to that morning as a man looks back to the beginnings of a ministry.

I was prepared to make those answers: in my publishing to let the Scriptures be sufficient as a basis for faith, to turn away from men's strange doctrines. My call was not to the pulpit, the sacraments, the vicarage; but to authors, manuscripts, booksellers.

Charles Gore in his charge to candidates on the eve of their ordination customarily asked: 'Tomorrow I shall say to you, "Wilt thou, wilt thou, wilt thou?" But there will come a day when another will say to you, "Hast thou, hast thou, hast thou?"'

My commission was positive, clear, wide-ranging. Another would one day say to me, 'Hast thou?' Although myself a stumbling disciple, I prayed for one gift: discernment. I sought to be able to recognise men on whom Christ had laid hold, whose hearts had responded to him, who could say with Paul, 'Let no man trouble me; I am the branded slave of the Lord Jesus.'

I left the Cathedral and stepped into the blaze of a June day, crossing to St. Paul's House, in Warwick Lane. The Dean of St. Paul's, Dr. Matthews, had laid the foundation

22

stone in July, 1962, and prayed: 'May the books that they publish spread light and understanding, hope and comfort; may they enrich the literature and culture of our land.'

# 3

# FIRST DAYS

The acceptance of a commission given in historic St. Paul's, on a spectacular mountaintop, or a dusty Damascus Road, does not guarantee that it will be carried out joyously, in the Spirit of Christ. That is the tragedy of righteous crusades; not the objectives, originally spontaneous and worthy, but the vain, repetitive and even cruel methods often employed. Men have seen visions, have heard the words of Christ, have known the call to adventure, but have gone forth with worldly weapons instead of spiritual power – to manipulate and not to win.

It would be my temptation.

As a beginner in publishing I looked to my senior colleagues for instruction: in the first place to Leonard Cutts, who as a noted religious editor was on intimate terms with writers of international repute. I expected him to pass on endless advice and exhortation. No one in London knew more about religious publishing, and about many other features of publishing, for he had also edited the popular Teach Yourself series with literally hundreds of titles, ranging from *Teach Yourself Typing* to *Teach Yourself Greek*. Legend had it that he edited these in bed. When else could he? He arrived in the office with the early morning cleaners, having cycled to his local railway station, refusing to drive a car or anything with an 'infernal combustion engine'.

An editor can learn about his function by examining past product and old correspondence, but when I turned to the filing cabinets I had a shock. They were arranged alphabetically, under authors, names I had previously seen only on book jackets: Geoffrey Bull, Donald Coggan, Elisabeth

Elliot, Stanley Jones, W. E. Sangster, Leslie Weatherhead. Think of a Christian author and the name was probably there.

But every file was empty.

Leonard, realising the confidential nature of hundreds of letters, and not wishing the past to weigh on his successor, had destroyed the correspondence which had accumulated, except for legally binding contracts which were lodged with Bill Gant, the royalties manager. I was dismayed. Today, I understand. The relationship between an author and his editor is as personal as that between a mother and an obstetrician. In a sense, an editor is the obstetrician of the publishing world. What authors shared with Leonard Cutts was for his eyes only.

With no correspondence to guide me, I turned to this experienced publisher for verbal advice. Hardly a situation had arisen with which he was unfamiliar. He had seen the public image and the private reality; the pitfalls, the opportunities, the topics which were popular, the subjects which brought in book reviews but few orders.

Leonard, before you retire, share it. Do you tell authors how to write? You reject poor books from unknown authors, but what happens when a well-established writer, sought after by other publishers, turns in an unsatisfactory book? Do you risk losing him? What if you've paid a substantial, non-returnable advance against royalties? Are there circumstances when you would accept the second-rate?

Leonard, how is it that you secured all those bestsellers, books which survived the years, with numerous reprints, with translations? What was your greatest publishing achievement and, in confidence, I will tell no one, your disaster? If you had threescore years and five to live again would you be a publisher?

I had observed that Leonard's letters were short, so short that he wrote them by hand, dispensing with a shorthand-typist. One paragraph was normal, two for a matter of complexity. Yet, they contained warmth and wisdom that made them treasured by the recipients. His verbal advice was equally brief. I recall only two specific instructions: the first negative, the second positive.

'Don't publish books for the World Council of Churches,' he said one afternoon.

I did not ask why. He may not have really meant it, but when a man gives an opinion so rarely you take note. There were other organisations he might have mentioned, but this one he singled out. I could not trace an unhappy publishing experience.

Publishers do not prosper, however by the books they do not publish, and Leonard's second counsel was concerned with successful religious publishing.

'Publish for the committed,' he said.

He did not know about my experience in St. Paul's. That had not been mentioned at Hodder. It was too private to talk about, hidden in my heart, but in telling me to publish for men with a commitment he was underlining my call to find those with a cause and a faith.

In the first raw days sitting behind an editor's desk I found few masterpieces among the trolley-load of unsolicited manuscripts that arrived in the office each morning. They were immaculately presented: typed on one side of the sheet only, in double-spacing, exactly as the textbooks advised. Each was scrutinised. One never knew. Most faltered at the first hurdle. As a bookseller I had learned to ask, 'Is there a customer for this?' Sophisticated editors, straight from university, pondered academic points, but unless this question could be answered in the affirmative there was no point in lengthy consideration. Publishing manuscripts for which there is no potential market puts bookseller and publisher out of business.

Manuscripts were returned, each with a personal letter, on the day they arrived. I learned this was unusual. Some publishers kept manuscripts for months to prove they had been read.

'The less time we spend on those we don't publish,' I told my secretary, 'the more we can give to those we do accept.'

'But you're not taking anything,' she protested.

For weeks every manuscript was returned. I was the most inexperienced publisher in London – and the most rapid rejector of manuscripts. I did not have the authority to accept a book but it was within my power to reject one and not to add to the thousands of titles which remained indefinitely on bookshop shelves, until one began to regard those shelves as literary cemeteries.

'Bishop Barry is downstairs and would like to see you,' the receptionist reported. I had not met F. R. Barry, who had retired after being Bishop of Southwell for twenty-two years, but his reputation was of a brilliant scholar and writer of distinction. Hodder had published three books by him: *Asking the Right Questions*, *Christian Ethics and Secular Society* and *The Atonement*.

I liked him immediately. He said he was never happier than when writing and that since his retirement he had written five books. He now planned the sixth, an autobiography to be called *Period of My Life*. Would Hodder like to publish?

I had looked at the sales of previous autobiographies written by bishops. There was no overseas market and British sales were limited. I wished that he had written in rather than calling, for I found it harder to say no face to face. Our conversation was troubled as he was extremely deaf and I had to shout to make myself heard. I remembered his contribution to the Anglican communion as a bishop and, before that, at Westminster Abbey and King's College, London.

'I'm very sorry, bishop, but I don't think it would be an economic publishing proposition.' Had he heard? 'I think we would prefer another volume like *Christian Ethics and Secular Society*.'

We shook hands and he left. Two days later I received a letter from him thanking us for our willingness to publish his autobiography. It meant a great deal to him. I took the letter to a senior colleague.

'Were you watching his hearing aid?' my colleague asked. He had edited his previous book. 'When he speaks he turns it on. Before you answer he turns it off.'

I laughed, unbelievingly.

'But what do I do?'

'The decent thing. He's a bishop. You send him a contract and publish it.'

It attracted good reviews. Although we did not clear all the edition, we sold sufficient to cover our printing costs. I did not share his liberal theology but I liked his honesty, his conviction that Christ is still the key to the human situation. He wrote:

Faith has had many an hour of doubt and darkness but the darkness has not overcome it . . . The foundation of faith is not in ideas, which must change with the changing movements of secular thought, but in the historical and living Person, yesterday and today and forever. Other foundation no man can lay. Apart from that Person the church has no existence . . . What we today call Christianity may undergo changes that we cannot envisage. What does not change is the irreducible Christ.

When I met him a few months before he died, his family stricken by a sudden, overwhelming tragedy, I was glad we had done the decent thing.

Religious publishing cannot survive on the writings of bishops and theologians. Too many books were being published for those in the pulpit and too few for those in the pew and outside the church.

Among the leading London publishers only Hodder and Collins were publishing Christ in paperbacks for the station bookstall. Hodder had been doing it since the 1930s with books like *For Sinners Only* by A. J. Russell and the C. F. Dempster series which sold hundreds of thousands. After the war Priscilla Collins, wife of Billy, who was chairman of Collins, persuaded her husband to buy up Geoffrey Bles so that the Fontana (now Fount) religious books could be launched with two key authors, C. S. Lewis and J. B. Phillips. Both companies shared a concern to find writers who could communicate in a language that people understood.

To publish in that language I must remain close to life as I had once known it as a young journalist, as I had experienced it in the bustle of London's West End. Soon I would be lunching with bishops, finding my way to Lambeth Palace, attending exclusive dinners. Christ is there but he is also resident in Coronation Street. Not all publishers go there.

I had the disadvantage of not being a scholar, and the good fortune of being a plain man.

After Harold Ross, first editor of the *New Yorker*, died Malcolm Muggeridge wrote:

> Ross had the great advantage, in an editor, of being largely illiterate. This meant that he wanted everything explained, and refused to pass a sentence not wholly comprehensible to him. It also meant that he instinctively distrusted pretentious, mannered writing, and, in matters of taste, followed his flair rather than any conformist (or anti-conformist) system.

In his early days John Wesley read his sermons to an old domestic servant, instructing her to interrupt when she could not understand. 'I design plain truth for plain people,' he said. 'I labour to avoid all words which are not easy to understand, all which are not used in common life; and, in particular, those kinds of technical terms that so frequently occur in Bodies of Divinity.'

I discovered that nine out of ten theologians wrote for the theologians or for reviewers. Communicating with ordinary men and women was of secondary importance. Lengthy attention in a specialist theological journal of limited circulation mattered more. I did not quarrel with this. Theology is 'the science of God'. They saw it as their duty, probably aptly, although one Cambridge theologian himself described the 'almost interminable theological argument, which has been as little enlightening as it has been little edifying'.

I liked the advice which C. S. Lewis gave to those who read such modern books: namely, never to allow yourself another new book till you have read an old one in between. If that is too much, you should at least read one old one to every three new ones. He saw the dangers of an exclusive contemporary diet. 'The only safety is to have a standard of plain, central Christianity ("mere Christianity" as Baxter called it) which puts the controversies of the moment in their proper perspective.'

Sadly, famous religious publishing houses had disappeared as warehouses filled with unappetising volumes by contemporary theologians. In London three went in a decade. In what has been called 'the battle for intelligibility' I looked in manuscripts for a Christ who would not be imprisoned in theological libraries but who strode beside common men speaking a common language, in a world of uncertainty and insecurity.

I did not turn away from theological books. Lewis insisted: 'If you do not listen to theology, that will not mean that you have no ideas about God. It will mean that you have a lot of wrong ones – bad, muddled, out-of-date ideas.' I turned my back on the obscure, the speculative, the unintelligible.

Our publishing would depend on discovering writers rather than reading manuscripts sent through the mail. The authors we needed must be found. Men like the Apostle Peter and women like Mary Magdalene who did not think in book terms, and writers like the Apostle Paul who rarely settled down to write unless they were in prison.

John wrote in his first Epistle of 'that which we have heard, which we have seen with our eyes, which we have looked upon and touched, concerning the word of life.' I prayed for writers who had heard, who had seen, who had looked upon and touched. 'I preached what I felt, what I smartingly did feel,' said Bunyan.

In the submissions I became familiar with the finer theological points which were being aired in academic circles, but the questions which they answered in seventy thousand words only a handful of readers asked.

There were other urgent questions that troubled men. Big, frightening ugly questions.

On a dull Friday morning, when I had been with Hodder for five months, one of them was asked in millions of homes as viewers saw pictures on their screens of the Aberfan disaster in Wales.

*Why didn't God save the children?*

# 4

# WHY GOD?

In a mining village in South Wales a man-made mountain of coal-slag – over a million tons – had slid remorselessly over terraced homes and cottages for one half mile to the Pantglas Junior School. Some of the children – all under eleven – having just finished morning prayers in the assembly hall, were in their classes standing for roll-call, laughing and talking, when the black avalanche came hurtling down upon them.

Television screens showed relatives and friends fighting against time to rescue the 160 victims of a twentieth-century Pompeii. Earth-moving equipment could not be used near the school. More rescuers were called for, otherwise it would take days to reach the children.

With two thousand other volunteers I went to Aberfan. I had never responded like this before. If God isn't there, I told myself, he isn't anywhere. I was troubled and perplexed. If the mountain had to move why not half an hour earlier before the kids arrived? Or a few hours later when half-term had begun? Why as they said their prayers?

On the train I took out some sausage rolls and offered one to an Indian sitting opposite. He was grateful and had settled back to eat it when his expression changed.

'If you don't mind,' he said handing it back with courtesy, 'but I'm a Muslim.'

'What do you think of this disaster?' I asked him when I had finished my roll. 'What does a Muslim say?'

'An act of God.' The reply came promptly, without the slightest hesitation. The train rattled on towards the Welsh valleys. 'Earthquakes, floods, typhoons, all come from God.'

31

'But surely,' I objected, 'you can't blame God for this. He didn't put that great slag-heap there. God didn't make that tip. The National Coal Board allowed tipping to go on above the village, and before that the mine owner. You can't blame the Almighty for that.'

'An act of God,' he insisted.

In a market town in Kent similar questions were being asked. More than 300 people were participating in a survey. 'Do you believe there is a God who cares for you?' they were asked. The answers that day were simple, straightforward. 'No, not after the Welsh disaster.'

As Aberfan came in sight I asked myself what answers were being given there to the agonising questions.

The road was choked with vehicles moving debris. I stumbled down the short hill and over the coalmine's waggon line. The noise was deafening. Drivers hunched wearily over their wheels. Along Aberfan Road a van pulled up outside Bethania Chapel. A line of policemen formed and tiny coffins were passed from hand to hand. Ten, fifteen, twenty: I gave up the terrible count.

I shook hands with the Reverend Kenneth Hayes, minister of Zion English Baptist Church. His own son, Dyfrig Hayes, was missing.

'You go into the Chapel and there are all these bodies very small, and you walk around dreading to find your own,' he said. 'My boy isn't there.'

Dyfrig's body was the 114th to be found.

'Let there be no bitterness,' said Mr. Hayes.

'I am lucky to have one little boy left,' his wife said. 'I try to be thankful for the nine beautiful years we have had. You can't own children. They are given to use – and taken away.'

I wanted to be among the rescuers but when I saw the pace I knew I would not earn my place. I could not keep up with the colliers. There were less dramatic jobs. Along the road Smyrna, the Baptist chapel, had been transformed into a casualty and refreshment centre. Cartons of apples from Kent had been stacked in the pulpit. Five hundred blankets had arrived from the Red Cross in London. The communion table was covered with white corrugated cardboard on which were placed cotton wool, Savlon, boracic

32

acid powder and other medical supplies. In the gallery miners, taking a break, stretched themselves out on pews. Mother's Pride bread was stacked on tabletops, while sandwiches by the hundred were being made by women from the Welfare Department of the Civil Defence. It was a church party – to which all had come in their oldest clothes, and dirtier than they had ever been.

'There can't be more survivors, not under all that, after all this,' an ambulance man said. Up to forty more children were still presumed buried but in the chaos no one knew. A woman who had lost two children burst out, 'There'll not be a child left in our street.'

A rescuer was taken to hospital. Another had been detained after a heart-attack, but no gap remained on the collapsed tip, the miners taking the brunt, refusing to rest, their hands blistered. Above Aberfan, within sight of the disaster, sheep grazed, lifting their heads to gaze stupidly at what had been their pasture land.

Within minutes of arriving on the tip men were covered with black slime. It was agonising, back-aching, most of all heartbreaking, because of what was found, and because of the children who remained to be found.

'What's that? Listen.' The word passed from man to man. Everyone around paused. 'From over there.' Those nearest stretched and bent and waited. There was no sound. There had not been for hours in that place. It was doubtful if there could be more survivors.

Torrential rain began to fall threatening to make the tip slide again and the rescuers were directly in its path. More men were summoned to build a wall of sandbags.

Digging had to stop at one point behind the school. 'There's a quarter of a million tons which could fall at any moment,' a fireman said. Every rescuer was warned. 'Be ready to run.'

An S.O.S. went out for rainwear. Puddles became lakes as drains were blocked. The group of parents outside the mortuary huddled closer. In the wet, the weariness became intolerable.

A walkie-talkie operator, high above the village, watched to give warning of any substantial earth movement. Officials knocked on doors and instructed househol-

33

ders to evacuate. Welfare services transferred to safer locations.

The rain washed down the black sludge. The tip began to move again, sliding inexorably, in minutes obliterating the work of hours of weary digging. The miners would have to start again.

After six hours it stopped raining. I knew how Noah must have felt but he was in the dry. It was almost unbelievable.

On Sunday morning the sun was shining. I cleaned up and left the hillside to attend the Zion English Baptist Church for the eleven o'clock service. It was to be conducted by Mr. Hayes.

A group of reporters and photographers were outside the door. A reporter held a *Sunday Mirror* with a bold headline: '*The Anger of the Church. Don't Blame God. Blame Stupid Men.*' It quoted the vicar of Aberfan, the Reverend Wilfred Jones. 'This terrible thing that has happened in our village has nothing to do with the wish or will of God. It was caused by man's stupidity and neglect, nothing else.'

The Wayside Pulpit, at the front of the church, declared: '*Thought for the Week. Trouble often gives opportunity to help.*'

A frail, elderly lady hesitantly entered the church and sat in a back seat. All the sorrow and heartbreak and loneliness of the village were portrayed in her slight form. I wanted to participate in the service as an act of worship, but I sensed that this morning I might be an intruder, so I slipped into the gallery, taking a hymnbook. A television camera team was already there.

At eleven a.m. there were three young boys and a girl in a white hat in the front row. Behind them a mother and two teenage daughters in slacks and woollen jumpers. An older woman with a green fur-trimmed coat sat praying.

Mr. Hayes went into the pulpit. He announced that the service of Holy Communion would not be held. There would be hymns, Bible reading and prayer but no sermon. There were now twenty-five people from the village in the congregation.

· 'Our numbers are small, but a tremendous lot of people are still working in the disaster.'

We stood to sing 'The Lord's my Shepherd', stumbling

over the lines, 'Yea, though I walk in death's dark vale, yet will I fear no ill.'

Mr. Hayes read from Psalm 90: 'Lord, thou hast been our dwelling place in all generations. Before the mountains were brought forth, or ever thou hadst formed the earth and the world, even from everlasting to everlasting, thou art God.' He turned to the magnificent words in Paul's Epistle to the Romans, Chapter 8: 'Who shall separate us from the love of Christ? Shall tribulation, or distress, or persecution, or famine, or nakedness, or peril, or sword? As it is written, for thy sake we are killed all the day long; we are accounted as sheep for the slaughter. Nay, in all these thing we are more than conquerors through him that loved us.'

His voice rose strongly: 'For I am persuaded, that neither death, nor life, nor angels, nor principalities, nor powers, nor things present, nor things to come, nor height, nor depth, nor any other creature, shall be able to separate us from the love of God, which is in Christ Jesus our Lord.'

The Reverend Keith Jones, in heavy leather boots and buff jacket, thinking of a close relative who had been taken to hospital after being rescued from a collapsed house, prayed for the bereaved and for those who were still digging. The sun was shining through the windows, the heavy trucks rumbled by, while the Taff flowed silently behind the church.

'Somewhere in the last twenty-four hours I've lost my handkerchief,' said Mr. Hayes as he stood in the pulpit. One was passed to him. 'Now is our chance to be the serving church.' He looked round the congregation, seeing them with fresh eyes. 'Let us thank God things are not worse. My only appeal is to the National Coal Board. Don't tip any more . . . Let us thank God for the miracles . . . We have now got to take the Word of God, a message of comfort.'

The final hymn was unwise. 'Safe in the arms of Jesus', was his choice, but he had to sit down at the end of the first verse and take out the borrowed handkerchief.

After the service a Sunday School teacher made a list of the dead and missing from the Sunday School. Her primary department had lost twelve children, and there were others missing in the senior schools. Meanwhile, in the church hall they were making tea and sandwiches for the lorry drivers. On the hillside the punishing slog continued. By Sunday evening 138 bodies had been recovered, and 118 had been identified. A few were still believed missing.

I was not present at the communal burial on Thursday. There was a cold wind and the sky was cloudy. Rain threatened once or twice. The funeral was timed for three p.m. but from nine a.m. the coffins were taken from the chapels to be slowly transported to the mountainside cemetery. Two eighty-foot long trenches had been prepared and above the trenches was a cross over a hundred feet tall made from flowers. The cross dominated the hillside. 'They died together, we want them to be buried together,' parents said.

Five weeks later I returned to Aberfan to gather material for *The Mountain that Moved*, which told from a Christian perspective of that week in Aberfan. The royalties were for the Save the Children Fund.

Had I found the answers to my questions? Well, in Aberfan they did not blame God, they blamed the National Coal Board. All over South Wales there were old coaltips full of potential and deadly danger. Repeated warnings had been ignored. Many felt bitter and enraged. At the opening of the inquest a father demanded that the cause of death be recorded as 'Buried alive by the National Coal Board'.

After a mine disaster in South Wales earlier this century someone wrote in bold letters for all who passed by to see:

Welsh Colliery Disaster
Where was God
There is no God.

'When a mountain moved, where was God?' I asked the local ministers. The Mayor's chaplain said, 'To us who falteringly seek to learn of Christ, came the discovery that we were meeting him in Aberfan, and doing so in the strangest places and often in the most unlikely people.'

'Faith isn't dead,' said the Methodist minister, 'but glows as a flickering flame to be coaxed and fed with friendship and kindness. I have been amazed at the receptiveness of

36

non-churchgoers whom we visited, the way prayer came naturally and was welcomed.'

'We in the church,' said the Baptist minister, 'have discovered there is more latent faith outside the Christian fellowship than we would have previously acknowledged.'

'We didn't find God in the disaster, but we found him in our distress,' said another. 'On that hillside the Cross of Christ assumed a fresh significance. It broke upon a few that Christ was identified with the agony, with the rescuers in intolerable conditions, with those who wept.'

Jim Ross, a Christian journalist, wrote:

These children who were buried by that man-made mountain were not alone. Christ was buried with them. The parents who stood outside a village chapel all night, shocked and shattered were not alone, for Christ shared their vigil. The men and women who fought without respite a shifting horror of muck and slime did not fight that thing alone. Christ was with them also in their filth and weariness and grief. When something like this Aberfan tragedy hits, that is the only strength: that Christ shared, suffered, died.

Shortly before his death, Dietrich Bonhoeffer said, 'It is only by living completely in this world that one learns to have faith . . . By this worldliness I mean living unreservedly in life's duties, problems, successes and failures, experiences and perplexities.'

During the tragedy in Aberfan the local chapels and churches lived in this world. 'The disaster exposed us and we must not go back to our isolation,' said one minister. 'We found Christianity was not simply serving God in a building.'

I found Aberfan a sombre place in which to contemplate Christian publishing. I saw that the answers might come from the theologians, but that the pertinent questions came from unbelievers. It was always so. At Jacob's well, Jesus being wearied with his journey sat and listened to the questions from the woman of Samaria. 'How is it?' she asked. 'From whence hast thou living water?'

'Why God?' demanded a father who had dug out the

37

body of his son, a teacher who had seen the village school disappear, a mother who sat up all night with a surviving child with recurring nightmares. Unless we harken to what they ask, they will not listen to us. But do we listen? Do we hear? Do we change the topic because we fear the inadequacy of our answer?

'Why God?' The question haunted me.

'Do not let me be a publisher,' I prayed, 'unless our books have something to say to those who go thirsty to the well for water.'

# 5

# NOT FOR BURYING

'Within our Christian convictions we hope never to reject the eternal gospel and its living literature. But we hope never to be afraid of new thinking, new dimensions, new voices, new language or new ways of fulfilling the vocation of the Christian publisher.' So wrote Paul Hodder-Williams, the chairman, on Hodder and Stoughton's centenary in 1968.

How should the centenary be marked? Hodder publish a complete range of literature from Enid Blyton's children's books, to Mary Stewart and John le Carré novels, with specialist divisions for educational, medical, technical and scientific books. Leonard Cutts persuaded the chairman and John Attenborough that the theme should be *One Hundred Years of Christian Publishing*. Other publishers were behaving like grave diggers with the death of God theology but in the absence of an official heavenly announcement we acted on the basis that God still reigned.

Dr. William Neil, of Nottingham University, penned a booklet telling the story of Hodder religious books. I was instructed to organise an exhibition in Stationer's Hall, London, opened by the Lord Mayor of London. There was a magnificent full-day conference for two hundred Christian booksellers, church bookstall managers and clergy, at which John Attenborough was the principal speaker. The celebrations were a notable success.

The second century of Hodder publishing started with a boom in Christian books. The sales graph shot upwards as it had not done since the 1930s. Turnover doubled. While academic publishers promoted titles like *The Death of God, Christian Atheism* and *Secular Christianity*, our faith in God's survival did not waver. After a couple of years the market for the death of God theologians collapsed. 'Buyers do not like to linger,' a cynic said, 'beside a corpse.'

Their arguments had been difficult for laymen to follow, but even theologians did not understand what other theologians were saying. Robert Blaikie, a New Zealand theologian on the Hodder list, wrote of the 'word-twisting, logic-flouting mental acrobatics' which 'cannot but issue in crippling confusion in the church, with a drastic loss of integrity in the use of theological words.'

C. S. Lewis told a magazine editor, Sherwood Wirt: 'A great deal of what is being published by writers in the religious tradition is a scandal and is actually turning people away from the church. The liberal writers who are continually accommodating and whittling down the truth of the gospel are responsible. I cannot understand how a man can appear in print claiming to disbelieve everything he presupposes when he puts on the surplice. I feel it is a form of prostitution.'

At the height of the 'let's bury God' publishing I met an extraordinary Christian, Pastor Richard Wurmbrand, who himself was no mean theologian. Pastor Wurmbrand, a converted Jew, had been released after fourteen years in Rumanian prisons. His faith was his crime. He had been kidnapped on February 29th, 1948 by secret police on his way to his Lutheran church. A van stopped in front of him. Four men jumped out and pushed him in. For years no one knew if he was alive or dead. Secret police, posing as released prisoners, told his wife they had attended his funeral.

In 1956, having been in prison for eight and a half years, he was unexpectedly released. He had been questioned *ad nauseam*, starved, brutally beaten, tortured but his captors had failed to destroy his faith.

After three and a half years of freedom he was imprisoned for a further five and a half years. Now he was strictly forbidden to preach to other prisoners. Whoever was caught doing this received a severe beating.

'A number of us,' he recalls, 'decided to pay the price for the privilege of preaching, so we accepted the terms. It was a deal: we preached and they beat us. We were happy

40

preaching. They were happy beating us.'

His wife, Sabina, had also been imprisoned for a time. Their nine-year-old son, Mihai, had been left to wander on the streets without mother or father. A woman risked her life and took him into her home.

One day Sabina read in a newspaper of an amnesty for political prisoners and hurried round to a friend's house to discuss the news. She prayed and returned to her own home, but had been in the house only five minutes when a neighbour came running. A telephone call had come through from an old friend who had been released that morning. He said the Pastor was on the list for that day. He had seen him waiting in the yard.

Sabina tried to go on peeling potatoes, but her heart was beating so fast she had to sit down. Hours passed. Another knock on the door and a neighbour on the floor below, who had a telephone, stood there smiling.

'There's a call for you,' she said. 'From out of town.'

Sabina hurried down and grabbed the receiver. It was Richard. When she heard his voice she fainted. When she came round they had brought down Mihai and he was speaking with his father who was still hundreds of miles away in the western provinces. He'd catch a train from the nearest station. But not today. His first underground church meeting had already been arranged for that evening.

He travelled on the overnight train and they met him at the station. She saw him before he saw her. He was thin and pale with a shaven head. The station rocked with the noise of greetings.

'Don't speak,' said Richard. 'Let me just look at you.'

'God has given you back to me,' she said.

In Oslo, Norway, Anutza Moise heard of his release. She had been a member of his church in Bucharest until 1948. With other persecuted Jews she had left Rumania and made her way to Norway but she had never forgotten the Pastor in whose home she had lived during an illness, or his beautiful wife.

Rumania was short of foreign currency and for ransoms had been known to release its citizens. Jews had been sold to Israel for £1,000 each. Anutza, with little money of her

41

own, contacted an organisation which assisted Jewish Christians; she wrote to the Norwegian Government and negotiated with the Red Cross, and with friends in Britain, France and Germany.

They were told that for Richard Wurmband the ransom was not £1,000 but £2,500. The money was raised. In December 1955 the Pastor with his wife and son arrived at her small home on the outskirts of Oslo. It was Christmas Eve. The snow was thick on the ground as Anutza dug up a Christmas tree to celebrate their freedom.

From that day he began a mission to alert the West about the thousands of Christians who had died in Communist countries, and to raise funds for the families of those who remained in labour camps.

Through a photograph of him in a church newspaper we had stumbled on a bestselling author who was to prove the most controversial, demanding, frustrating and lovable religious writer we would encounter. For years hardly a day passed without a letter from him; two letters were commonplace when he could not sleep. Everything about him was giant-size, including the files in our office.

On his first visit to our London office he gave us his book *Tortured for Christ*. He stipulated that it must be published within six weeks. We normally took nine months to print and launch a book. We did it in six weeks. There was no time for editing or proof-reading. It mattered little. It sold a total of two million copies in twenty-three languages. More than 100,000 readers responded by writing to him.

'I am a man who has never seen a book in fourteen years,' he told us as he looked around at the volumes in our showroom. Hodder were publishing about 600 new titles a year and had some 6,000 different titles on the backlist in print. 'I almost never had a pencil in my hand for fourteen years . . . I am only a man. When you sleep – I can't sleep, because I hear what is happening there. When I go to church, you hear the song; I hear the cries of the tortured martyrs.'

His life was in danger. He had been threatened as a result of his disclosures in the West about the persecution and imprisonment of Christians in Eastern Europe. Before he left Rumania, when the ransom money had been paid, he

42

was interviewed by the secret police.

'Now you may leave Rumania. You may preach about Christ as much as you like, but don't touch us!' he was warned. 'If you touch us, for a thousand dollars we can find a gangster who will finish you, or we can bring you back to Rumania.' They added one more threat. 'Or we can destroy your reputation by stories of immorality. Be careful what you do.'

He crossed roads warily, fearful that a car might intentionally run him down. At the top of Ludgate Hill we looked three or four times before stepping out together. The anxiety might have been groundless but it was real. When we invited him to lunch and he realised a lady editor, Myrtle Powley, would be present, he insisted on bringing his wife, Sabina. He had seen how the Communists destroy the reputation of Christian pastors.

No attempt was made on his life. The authorities in Eastern Europe had more subtle methods. They circulated documents which stated he had been in prison for currency offences and not for his faith. I received from Rumania a fat dossier, addressed to me by name, which claimed: 'Wurmbrand's mental disorders lead him to irresponsible and illogical manifestations which are revealing of his sickly mind.'

I shared them with the Hodder and Stoughton directors. They had lunched with the man and had no doubts but, as I was going to Scandinavia, they agreed I should call on Anutza Moise in Oslo. The snow was deep on the ground as on the Christmas Eve when the Wurmbrand family turned up on her doorstep. She was able to reassure me and later to introduce me to others who had been in prison with the Pastor, or who had worshipped in his church.

I saw a great deal of the Pastor when he visited Britain to preach and lecture. He shared with me the agony of solitary confinement in a cell thirty feet below ground, when he had not seen sun, moon or stars, flowers or snow, or any other man except for the guards and interrogators, who beat him. He passed the hours in spiritual exercises.

'Each night I prepared a fresh sermon,' he said.

'But you had no congregation. No paper, no books, not even a pencil.'

43

'I preached to God,' he said. 'On other nights I imagined that my church members came to visit me, or that the children were there. Sometimes I prepared a sermon for my own soul.'

He memorised the sermons by putting the outlines into verse. Preachers don't waste sermons. He kept the memory of them alive by continual repetition and when he was released he wrote down 350 outlines.

Books of sermons rarely sell, but we asked him to send a selection of these sermons for consideration. When they came we saw we had treasure. Had sermons like these ever been published? They were the outpourings of a man whose pillars of reason had rocked under strain; who at times was near to apostasy; who had known not only physical but extreme spiritual tension, the peak of suffering.

He wrote a preface to *Sermons in Solitary Confinement*: 'I have lived in exceptional circumstances and passed through exceptional states of spirit. I must share these with my fellow men.' The first sermon, 'God's Unjust Laws' was addressed to God. 'With you,' he told God, 'I can be absolutely frank. You have no inquisition. You will not try me for heresy. In front of other people I had to praise you. Here I am free to question you, and to reproach you, as David and Job and others have done. I will tell you everything in my heart.'

We sent the manuscript to Dr. J. B. Phillips for assessment. He confirmed our view. It was, he said, astonishing, perhaps the most astonishing book he had read, adding that Richard Wurmbrand must surely be one of the most remarkable Christians living today.

'Most of us,' Dr. Phillips went on, 'I am sure would have gone out of our minds in a matter of weeks if not days. But here we have a man who though beaten and tortured by day spent many of his night hours in prayer and in composing and committing to memory some 350 sermons. Some are naïve with the innocence of a child. Some seem like the workings of a mind driven insane with pain and drugs. Yet one is driven to the conclusion that the apparent madness is not unlike what Paul once called, in a bold and inspired moment, "the foolishness of God". I have long suspected,

44

and feared, the only answers to the human predicament are discovered under the terrible pressures of human agonies where they meet and are met by the unimaginable agony of God.'

One sermon, 'The pain of erotic imagination', considered the distress of sexual suffering. On the advice of friends it was omitted, but later it was included in another volume. The advisors, good men, were reluctant to accept that part of his torment.

'I don't know what is happening to me now,' it read. 'It may be that they put aphrodisiacs in our food. The fact is, I cannot defend myself against erotic fantasy . . . I must learn to accept even these erotic imageries.' From his own experience he passed to a new understanding of what he called 'one of the greatest sufferings of mankind. So many beautiful souls cannot find a suitable partner; others are sick.' He concluded: 'So let us remain serene, even through these tormenting imaginings from which, in a different measure, many of you also suffer. Christ is with you in these things, too.'

We booked the Royal Festival Hall, London, to launch *Sermons in Solitary Confinement* and dignitaries like the Dean of St. Paul's graced the platform. It was a triumphant two hours. Richard Wurmbrand's presence was a reminder of the suffering church. And a reminder that Communism could not obliterate Christianity.

'There are not enough shovels on earth to bury the truth,' he said.

Pastor Wurmbrand had a unique experience of God in prison but that did not make him infallible. He was impatient with organisations which did not respond to his challenge to give up their calling to proclaim the desperate situation of the underground church. He made tens of thousands of friends and a few enemies. In his fervour he was not as precise as an editor expects. When I received more demands from him than were justified: when he was dissatisfied that our subsidiary rights manager, Clare Bristow, had negotiated only twenty-three translations of *Tortured for Christ*, when his letters occupied the entire drawer of a filing cabinet, then I looked at the photograph in my office, a prison picture, of a shrunken body and haggard face, and recalled the solitary cell he had occupied with angels.

He was a powerful demonstration that an obituary of God was premature. I refused to put a halo round his head, but I would have walked miles to sit at his feet.

Sometimes I felt a hypocrite. It was profitable to be his publisher: every month we were printing a new edition of one of his books. My reputation was being established within the company at the expense of such experience. But would my faith have survived the solitary confinement, and torture, the prolonged separation from family and church? After fourteen years would I have been able to speak of the adventure of God, of life's choices, of the Lordship of Christ? If all I had was a bed with a straw mattress, a blanket, a bucket in the corner, and a tin mug, would I be able to believe in the promises of God?

It was easier to be a publisher than a prisoner.

# 6

# THE DREAM

Sometimes God's signals take us by surprise. When we want to go they say wait; when we want to wait, or stop, they say go.

I saw this demonstrated in the life of Dr. Martin Luther King. For him the signal came unexpectedly one December afternoon.

Martin, a young Baptist minister, had studied for his degree of Doctor of Philosophy in systematic theology, and was beginning a pastoral ministry caring for his church members. He saw years of preaching and visiting ahead, with opportunity for further study. At three o'clock one Monday he attended a small protest meeting and was asked, 'Will you be our President?'

The invitation was a surprise. He did not want to be the president of anything. Three weeks earlier he had refused a similar request. His first child had been born days before. He was needed at home. The baby girl was cooing and cuddly and trustful and loving. He could barely wait for the meeting to end.

God sent him a signal. An inner voice prompted him, in spite of his personal wishes, to accept. 'If you think I can serve, I will,' he said.

Within a few hours he found himself addressing 4,000 black citizens. Soon the threatening telephone calls started. A bomb was thrown into his front porch, the living-room windows shattered. His preacher-father advised him to withdraw: 'Better be a live dog than a dead lion.'

Thirteen years later he died of a gunshot wound in his neck. 'God,' his family said, 'had thrust something upon him and he did not turn away.'

47

His life became an inspiration to me. When I arrived at Hodder, he was planning his fourth book, *Chaos or Community*, and I was asked to be his London editor. British sales of his titles had been slow, although he had captured the imagination of millions, including Paul Hodder-Williams.

Martin went to Jamaica where, working sixteen hours a day, he completed his manuscript in six weeks. I read it and prepared an appraisal for the directors. I outlined the content and glowed, but then I pointed out that the previous books had barely made economic sense. I found it hard to make a strong recommendation to publish. I sat on the fence.

If I had been in publishing longer, I would have known that some books should be published at all costs. And they are. The Board would see the figures, ponder the estimates, then determinedly put the calculations aside. All quality publishers do so.

'Publish with enthusiasm,' Paul Hodder-Williams scribbled on my report. The other directors supported him.

Publication was fixed for the last Monday in March, 1968. Early that month I sent advance copies to Dr. King telling him of our publicity plans and asking if a visit to Britain was imminent. Television, radio and the national press sought interviews. I did not mention signing sessions. He had been stabbed while autographing books in an American store.

His presence in London would double the sales. The book would be in the bookshops but we needed Martin Luther King headlines to move them out.

I received no reply but we had the headlines.

On Thursday night, April 4th, I turned on the radio. With millions of listeners worldwide I heard that he had been assassinated at the Lorraine Motel in Memphis. He was standing on the balcony, ready to go out for dinner, when there was a shot. It sounded like a firecracker.

Demand soared for *Chaos or Community*. Paperback and serial rights were sold. But there was sorrow in the office. With the rest of the world we were stunned and appalled at the atrocity.

In 1969 we received the typescript of his widow's book,

*My Life with Martin Luther King, Jr.* Correta Scott King had placed the manuscript with a literary agency and to our dismay we found that copies had been sent by the agent to a number of publishers for an 'auction'. It would apparently go to the highest bidder. I was asked to make an assessment.

On a perfect August day, to escape from the telephone and other distractions, I spent the morning and afternoon reading the typescript in the pleasant gardens adjacent to St. Paul's. A few holiday-makers were resting in the shade, or stretched out on lawns, the sparrows hopped around in search of crumbs, but I was across the Atlantic.

I had been whisked away to Atlanta's Ebenezer Baptist Church, to Correta's own home in Alabama, where her father's saw-mill was burned to the ground; I walked on the long marches, and witnessed the imprisonments and the tragic end. I saw demonstrated in one man's life all the principles of adventure I had read about in *The Adventure of Living*.

I finished the typescript and, praying for a measure of the courage and faith which marked the man, recommended to the chairman the payment of a substantial advance against future earnings.

To secure the rights he doubled that figure.

'We have lost money on bad books,' the chairman said, 'and sometimes on run-of-the-mill books. Now this is a great book. Let's put in an offer they can't refuse, the largest advance we have offered in the history of the company.'

The offer was made and accepted. The fact that sales, though big, never justified the total advance, was accepted without a quibble by the directors.

A record of Dr. King speaking is playing as I write these words. It reminds me of the lessons we can learn from him: of the situation which a man commonly faces who dares to make God's dream his own, who responds to God's signal.

*The dream might not be a personal choice, but a burden accepted*.

On December 1st, 1955, Mrs. Rosa Parks, riding home from work in Montgomery, was one of four Negroes ordered to give up their seat for white passsengers. Her feet

49

were tired and she refused. The other Negroes moved but she was booked at the local police station for violating Montgomery's segregation laws. Dr. King showed his displeasure by joining a boycott of the buses. Leaflets were circulated, 'Don't ride to work, to town, to school, or any place, Monday, 5th December.' On that same Monday Mrs. Parks was fined ten dollars and four dollars costs. That afternoon Dr. King accepted the presidency of the newly-formed Montgomery Improvement Association.

'There comes a time,' he said, 'when people get tired. We are here to say to those who have mistreated us so long that we are tired – tired of being segregated and humiliated, tired of being kicked about by the brutal feet of oppression . . . Our actions must be guided by the deepest principles of our Christian faith. Love must be our regulating ideal.'

Those who heard Dr. King that Monday evening knew they had found a leader, but he remained pastor of the Dexter Avenue Baptist Church for five years. Like Moses he had told God he was not the man, that there were elements who would never listen to him, but when he tendered his resignation as pastor he recognised that he was not faced with a personal choice, but a burden laid upon him by God, the God who cares for the dispossessed and under-privileged.

*The dream will inevitably provoke opposition.* It did for Dr. King. It will for each of us. There were Negroes who were opposed to his policy of non-violence and there were Christian ministers who said, 'We strongly urge our Negro community to withdraw support from these demonstrations.'

Dr. Billy Graham, 'a good personal friend', advised him 'to put the brakes on a little' and encourage a 'period of quietness in which moderation prevails'. 'Go slow, Dr. King', became a slogan.

*The dreamer will know periods of doubt when he will wish to withdraw.* One of his friends, William Robert Miller, tells how after one threatening telephone call Dr. King got out of bed and went down to the kitchen to brood over a cup of coffee.

'How can I get out of this without looking like a coward?' he prayed aloud. 'I am here taking a stand for what I believe

50

is right. But now I am afraid. The people are looking to me for leadership. I am at the end of my powers. I have nothing left. It's come to the point where I can't face it alone.' In that hour Miller tells us that Dr. King felt a resurgence of energy and inner peace. A voice seemed to be saying to him, 'Stand up for righteousness, stand up for truth, and God will be at your side for ever.'

When a bomb was thrown into his doorway about a thousand men and women demonstrated their loyalty by surrounding the house ready for action. 'Stop,' Dr. King said. 'We must meet hate with love. Jesus still cries across the centuries, "Love your enemies".'

He had discovered the cost of leadership. 'A man's worth is measured by his commitment,' he would say.

*The dreamer may gain recognition and honour.* It is his most vulnerable period. Dr. King was awarded the Nobel Peace Prize in 1964. His contribution was acknowledged with the world's highest humanitarian award. 'I feel as though this prize has been given to me for something that has *not* yet been achieved,' he said. 'It is a commission to go out and work even harder for the things in which we believe.'

He passed through London on the way to Oslo and preached in St. Paul's Cathedral. He took a familiar theme. 'Set yourself earnestly to discover what you are made to do and then give yourself passionately to the doing of it.' Dr. King's father, carried away by the sermon, was muttering under his breath a favourite phrase which he would have shouted out in his home church. 'Make it plain, son, make it plain.' His son made it plain. After the service, Dr. Wand, an old and famous British bishop, came to him and grasping his hand said, 'I am an old man, Dr. King, but I am glad I lived long enough to hear that sermon.'

When he returned to America he was given a hero's welcome. Fireboats jetted streams of water on the Hudson River. In Washington he was invited with his wife to the White House to meet the President and Vice-President, and, most special of all, in Atlanta the members of the Ebenezer Church gave a reception in Fellowship Hall. These were the home folk who shared with him this pinnacle of recognition. It was gay and glorious.

51

*Men will kill the dreamer if they cannot kill the dream.* He was thirty-nine when he was assassinated. At his funeral the marches in Montgomery, Birmingham, Selma, Chicago, and other cities were recalled; his contribution to abolishing segregation in downtown establishments, to the passage of the civil-rights legislation in 1964 and 1965; his belief that one day none will be denied because his skin is black and none favoured because his eyes are blue.

The sermon at the funeral service was given by Benjamin E. Mays, President of Morehouse College in Martin's student days.

'This man was loved by some and hated by others,' he said. 'If any man knew the meaning of suffering, Dr. King knew. House bombed; living day by day for thirteen years under constant threats of death; maliciously accused of being a Communist; falsely accused of being insincere and seeking the limelight for his own glory; stabbed by a member of his own race; slugged in a hotel lobby; jailed over twenty times; occasionally deeply hurt because friends betrayed him – and yet this man had no bitterness in his heart, no rancour in his soul, no revenge in his mind.'

An associate paid this tribute: 'When an assassin's bullet ended Martin Luther King's life it failed in its purpose. More people heard his message in four days than in the twelve years of his preaching.'

Correta Scott King came to London for publication of the biography and for four days I escorted her and talked about Martin. She arrived at London's Heathrow airport at one thirty a.m. and after a few hours' sleep the activity started, beginning with a party at Robin Denniston's London home with Bishop Trevor Huddleston. There were television interviews and a magnificent press conference in Stationer's Hall; a visit to No. 10, Downing Street to meet the Prime Minister, and a luncheon which the directors asked me to organise for four hundred people at Quaglino's in St. James. Among the guests was the Archbishop of Canterbury, Dr. Michael Ramsey.

Correta is a professional singer and gave her first public concert in Ohio in 1948; she sang regularly in the choir of Ebenezer and has given a Freedom Concert in New York City's Town Hall. At the last minute I asked if she would sing after her speech at the luncheon.

No one at that luncheon will forget her bravery, her conviction, but it was her singing which brought us to our feet. The applause was tumultuous. She demonstrated her belief that with music she had a means of communication more powerful and effective than either speaking or singing alone.

But we were not only applauding her singing; we were saying thank you to the man who dared to dream, who responded to God's signal, who gave his life to others . . . to love somebody, to feed the hungry, to clothe the naked, to visit those who were in prison, to serve humanity, to do his duty as a Christian, to spread the message the Master taught.

When I saw Correta off at London Airport she autographed a copy of her book for me and gave me a photograph of herself. On the back it said:

> The amazing and wonderful and terrible things that came later in our lives created no problems between us. I had decided I would become the wife of Martin Luther King, Jr., and though I could not foresee what the future held – his leadership of the Civil-Rights Movement, the work and the strain, the dangers, his fame, and the tragedy – there was never a moment that I wanted to be anything but the wife of Martin Luther King.

Recently I returned from a visit with my wife to the home in Atlanta, 501, Auburn Avenue, where Martin was born and lived for the first twelve years of his life. It is now included in the five-block Martin Luther King, Jr. Historical District, which also incorporates Ebenezer Baptist Church, his spiritual home, as well as his grave adjacent to the church. Throughout his life, memories of important youthful events and happy times in the 'house on Auburn' were etched in Martin's memory.

We saw the original furnishings, including the family piano bequeathed to the home by his mother, whose accurate memories facilitated the authentic restoration of the living room and the bedroom in which Martin was born. Even the wallpaper was matched to 'Mamma' King's recol-

53

lections, to make the restored home as near as possible to the way it was.

There are thousands of monuments to war. This is a monument to non-violence. There are thousands of monuments to white men. This is a national memorial to a black man. Every year 200,000 visitors travel to see the home and the church in Atlanta, concerned to perpetuate his dream for a world united in justice, equality, human dignity and peace.

His best monument is not the house, however, but the changed attitudes which today exist between white and black in Southern cities like Atlanta. Our taxi driver confirmed this for us, but we saw it with our own eyes.

For me the visit was a pilgrimage. I was able to obtain recordings of his speeches, to hear again that marvellous voice.

Everybody can be great. Because everybody can serve. You don't have to have a college degree to serve. You don't have to make your subject and your verb agree to serve. You don't have to know about Plato and Aristotle to serve. You don't have to know Einstein's Theory of Relativity to serve. You don't have to know the second theory of thermo-dynamics in physics to serve. You only need a heart full of grace. A soul generated by love.

# 7

# THE NICODEMUS
# EXPERIENCE

'If God were to take the Holy Spirit out of our midst today,
about ninety-five per cent of what we are doing in our
churches would go on, and we would not know the difference.' The words of Dr. Carl Bates have been widely
quoted. Before asking, 'Was that true of my church', I
asked, 'Is that true of me?' Would ninety-five per cent of
those things which I did remain unchanged if God were to
take the Holy Spirit from me? Would I, would my compan-
ions, would the booksellers know the difference? Was I
relying on flair, on being astute, discerning, a good
businessman? Or on the Holy Spirit?

Luke begins his second book, The Acts of the Apostles,
by telling us that what Jesus began to do and teach he now
continues through the Holy Spirit. His Gospel was concerned with Jesus in the flesh, his second book with what he
did through the Spirit in the ministry of the church. It was
still the work of Jesus.

I would like to have been Dr. Luke's publisher! He was
the first biographer of St. Paul. I was 2,000 years too late to
be able to offer him a publishing contract. Instead, my role
was to be a publisher of the work of Jesus through the Holy
Spirit in the twentieth century. If you like, further volumes
in *The Acts of the Holy Spirit*.

Hodder allowed me to do this. A denominational publisher, with its advisory board, would have wanted to look
over my shoulder. Warnings would have been issued: he's
Catholic, he's charismatic, he's a Calvinist, he's not
evangelical, he's not an Anglican. The 'he's not one of us' is

a stumbling block in religious publishing, endeavouring to confine the Holy Spirit to 'our synagogue', to 'our upper-room'. The Holy Spirit will not be contained. The early church had to make that reluctant discovery.

I had my share of prejudice, but in my publishing I prayed for unblinkered eyes: to see the ministry of the Spirit whether in a cathedral, a meeting of the Christian Brethren, a Welsh chapel, a Roman Catholic convent, a Salvation Army hall, or completely outside structured Christianity.

'Where would you expect to find Jesus if he came to London this Christmas?' I asked a Salvation Army officer. 'He would go to one of those posh Park Lane hotels,' she said, 'and sit in the empty chair by the lonely lady in furs nursing her poodle.'

Dr. James S. Stewart was a former Moderator of the General Assembly of the Church of Scotland, and for twenty years Professor of New Testament Language, Literature and Theology in the University of Edinburgh. I recall reading his manuscript *Wind of the Spirit*, which demonstrated that as no man can control the wind or dictate its direction, so no man, no church, can domesticate the Spirit of God or limit his sphere of operation.

He wrote of Nicodemus on the Mount of Olives, the wind blowing up from the valley stirring the branches and rustling the leaves of the olive trees. Jesus was speaking to Nicodemus about the work of God in the life of the soul but Nicodemus, a theologian, did not understand. So Jesus made it simple.

'Listen to the wind, Nicodemus! Listen to the wind! You can hear its sound – the night is full of it, hark to it in the tops of the trees – but where it has come from and where it is going no man knows. Now, Nicodemus, the Spirit of God is just like that – invisible yet unmistakable, impalpable yet full of power, able to do wonderful things for you if only you will stand in its path and turn your face to it and open your life to its influence.'

Dr. Stewart spoke of the ceaseless action of the Spirit – 'the wind bloweth'. Never has there been a time when the Spirit of God has not been actively at work. He spoke of the sovereign freedom of the Spirit – 'the wind bloweth where

56

it listeth'. He referred to the indisputable evidence of the Spirit – 'thou hearest the sound thereof'. When the wind is blowing, it makes its presence felt. When the Spirit of God stirs up a church or an individual there is evidence of his working. He went on to describe the inscrutable origin of the Spirit – 'but canst not tell whence it cometh'. With all great movements of the Spirit one asks where they have sprung from. Finally he mentioned the incalculable destiny of the Spirit – 'canst not tell whence it cometh and whither it goeth'. You cannot tell where he is liable to carry you.

What a directive for Christian publishing, I thought. Listening for where the Spirit of God is at work, looking for the indisputable evidence of a stirring in a community, a church, a preacher, a writer.

I was to give a talk to an international Christian publishers' conference. The unspoken desire of each publisher, whether from Europe, America, Australia, New Zealand, Africa or Asia, was to find good books, hopefully titles which sold 100,000 copies instead of 3,000. They expected me to talk about contracts, foreign rights, jacket design, publicity, the Hodder experience. I startled them by talking about the Nicodemus experience, taking them to the Mount of Olives.

'Let's stop imitating each other and start listening,' I said. I told them how the Hodder chairman had likened publishing to a game of cricket. Cricket was a constant topic in the dining-room. A player took a catch and the batsman was out. The player was tempted to remain standing in the identical spot. Publishers, he said, made the same mistake. A catch was made, a bestseller emerged, and the publishers rushed to that spot. Where there had been no one suddenly there would be a crowd. 'But the ball rarely drops in the same spot twice,' he said.

It happens in religious publishing. Every conference delegate saw that. A glut of books on drugs, the Jesus people, missionary martyrs, the death of God, or volumes of contemporary prayers weakly imitating those of Michel Quoist. Publishers watching other publishers.

I quoted to them from John's Gospel, Chapter 3. Jesus said, 'Listen. Thou hearest its sound, but canst not tell whence it cometh or whither it goeth.' Great books? We

57

cannot tell whence they cometh. In the words of Dr. Stewart, what we have to do is to get our sails up, now that the wind is here.

At question time I sympathised with some editors. They were committee controlled. It is difficult to get a committee to listen to the wind. They are disturbed by other sounds, wondering where it blew yesterday; or they are distracted, as Nicodemus might have been, by the moon riding high over Jerusalem.

Fifteen years ago there were few publishers in Britain who would publish a charismatic book. There was almost a conspiracy among Christian publishers and booksellers to keep quiet about this fresh recognition of the Holy Spirit. They were worried by what they saw as similarities to old-style Pentecostalism, with its prayers which bordered on ecstasy and lack of ministerial formality.

When Leonard Cutts, before my arrival, published Michael Harper's book, *As at the Beginning*, it was 'under the counter' in most Christian bookshops. Leonard Cutts had taken a courageous decision. The author had been on the staff of All Souls, Langham Place, until 1964, when he had left to start the process which led to the creation of the Fountain Trust. It was common knowledge that John Stott, the Rector, did not share Michael's view. There was a difference on theology. John Stott did not suggest his curate should leave the church, although he was under some pressure from others to do so. Nor was Michael Harper critical of All Souls. 'While other churches were reporting shrinking congregations,' he wrote, 'All Souls maintained its momentum, the ability and leadership of John Stott playing a large part in this.'

Michael Harper's book manuscript, *Walk in the Spirit*, arrived in the office shortly after my appointment. It told of the miraculous powers which marked the early days of the Christian church.

Since 1962 we have been meeting hundreds of Christians who testify to a revolution in their lives . . . The purpose of this book is to try to help those who have come into touch with the new dimension . . . Thank God, we are seeing in our day the renewal of spiritual power in the

58

lives of many Christians. It is springing from the recognition by many that we do not know the Holy Spirit as we should, and that it is possible, indeed imperative, to be filled with the Holy Spirit, and led by him as the early Christians were.

The manuscript posed a problem. Since Leonard Cutts had accepted *As at the Beginning*, the division between those represented by the author and those for whom John Stott was a gracious spokesman had widened. Stott's *Your Confirmation* had sold more than 100,000 copies on the Hodder list. I did not want to offend the Rector of All Souls, my former colleagues in Scripture Union, nor the authors I sought to attract to the list. Noted Anglican clerics had expressed concern with the emphasis on 'the baptism in the Holy Spirit' and 'speaking in tongues', afraid of the danger of seeking the gifts instead of the Giver. Afraid too, I suspected, of seeing control pass from the clergy.

We would publish their views. Should we also provide a platform for writers like Michael Harper? For those, in his words, who 'either on their own in private prayer, or in company with others through the laying-on of hands, are being filled with the Spirit, and often speaking in another language as the disciples did on the day of Pentecost.'

I sent *Walk in the Spirit* to an outside reader, a distinguished cleric. He advised against publication unless there was considerable revision. I next consulted a reader who had favoured Hodder publishing the author's first book. 'Don't,' he said. 'Things have changed. The renewal movement is probably finished.'

Letters from two leading ministers, one Anglican, one Free Church, gently advised me that this Neo-Pentecostal movement was causing division among Christians. 'Like the Reformation?' I was tempted to ask, but my respect for them was too great. They were balanced men, fine Christians.

Michael Harper waited patiently, troubled that my appointment would terminate his association with Hodder, wondering if, with a Scripture Union background, I would be more cautious than his friend Leonard Cutts who had first sought him out.

59

The temptation was to play it safe along with other publishers. Hodder was associated with the Establishment: with a long succession of archbishops and bishops, learned deans and busy canons of cathedrals, sometimes venturing into nonconformist waters with champions like Leslie D. Weatherhead and W. E. Sangster. Michael Harper had no church appointment now. Little visible means of support. The Fountain Trust had no members. People who attended their meetings and conferences were told that they should go back to their home churches and find their fellowship there. It did not have funds to buy a quantity of the book if we published it.

I remembered, however, my commission on that June morning, my first day at Hodder, in St. Paul's Cathedral. What had God said to me? 'Publish for the whole church of Jesus Christ. For all men who truly believe that Jesus is the Son of God, who know him as Lord.' 'For charismatics, Lord?' I had distinctly asked the question. 'For charismatics,' was the answer.

Michael was part of a great movement of the Spirit which had not ended but had burst forth into fresh life. His experience would take him around the world, often with his musical wife, Jeanne, building bridges between the denominations as men and women found a new confidence in an ever-present Lord through the Holy Spirit.

With the blessing of the directors, I wrote and told him that Hodder and Stoughton would be honoured to publish *Walk in the Spirit*. It went into five printings, was published in America and translated into other languages. It was followed by books like *Spiritual Warfare*, *None can Guess*, *Glory in the Church*, *A New Way of Living*, *Let my People Grow*, and *Bishop's Move*. His name on our list attracted men of similar calibre and enabled us to launch songbooks like *Sound of Living Waters*, *Fresh Sounds* and *Cry Hosanna*, which sold scores of thousands of copies.

Years later I learned that John and Elizabeth Sherrill, co-authors with David Wilkerson of *The Cross and the Switchblade* had found Christian publishers in America equally nervous about this Holy Spirit movement. The climax of their book emphasised the Pentecostal aspect of David Wilkerson's ministry.

'The charismatic renewal,' David Wilkerson wrote, 'had not yet become acceptable; we were still living in a day when Pentecostals were considered Holy Ghost bumpkins.'

John and Elizabeth Sherrill had spent fourteen months on research and then had gone through six different rewrites of the book. They had literally prayed over each page of *The Cross and the Switchblade* as it was written, little dreaming they were writing a world bestseller.

Eventually, they found a secular New York publishing house to take on the book. The proprietor, who understood little about it, told them to write about the baptism in the Holy Spirit with complete honesty. He advised well. Hundreds were brought into a new experience through reading about it. The book sold eleven million copies in a total of twenty-five languages.

When Christian ears are closed to the wind of the Spirit God uses other ears. Bernard Geis, who published *The Cross and the Switchblade*, is a Jew.

# 8

# MUSHROOMS

I became the editor in charge of all religious publishing after Leonard's departure. No appointment could have given me greater pleasure. 'I'd rather be religious editor than the chairman or a bishop,' I told friends. Dr. Donald Coggan, then Archbishop of York, confirmed my judgment. He delivered his typescript, *Prayers of the New Testament*, and asked over a lunch given by Paul Hodder-Williams whether I would consider swopping jobs with him. An exhilarating prospect for a layman: if I had known he was going to Canterbury I might have said yes! With a concern for disseminating Christian literature evident in his speeches and his involvement in the Feed the Minds Campaign, he liked the idea of being a publisher.

'When you sell a man a book,' he quoted Christopher Morley, 'you do not sell him just twelve ounces of paper, ink and glue; you sell him a whole new life.' He later wrote, 'We need to capture the imagination of the best graduates of our universities, with the possibility of feeding the minds of millions with the message of Christ.'

Archbishops, I found, can relax. When he was leaving our offices I offered him an advance copy of a scholarly religious title to read on the train from King's Cross to York. He had finished an exhausting week in London and looked disappointed. 'Have you a novel, a thriller?' he asked. He spotted a John Creasey title on the shelf. 'Would you recommend that?'

'I recommend all our books, Archbishop.'

It was not true. In the spring of 1970 I found myself publicly disassociating myself from one title, an unfortunate publication by John Allegro entitled *The Sacred*

*Mushroom and the Cross.*

The bizarre story began for me when Robin Denniston told me he had been to Manchester the previous day to see John Allegro, a lecturer in Old Testament and Intertestamental Studies at Manchester University. John Allegro had been the first British representative on an international editing team preparing the Dead Sea Scrolls for publication.

'I'm sending him a contract,' Robin said, naming a substantial sum to be paid by way of advance against future royalties.

'Another Dead Sea scroll discovery?' I asked.

'Not quite. It's really about sacred mushrooms. He's been researching an ancient fertility cult and its relationship to the Old Testament.'

The book would be by a scholar for scholars. The author's previous book, *The Dead Sea Scrolls*, published in 1956, had sold 250,000 copies. I had seen it in the bookshops but I did not know, and I doubt if Robin did, that when it was issued a group of fellow scholars had published a letter in *The Times* disassociating themselves from it. A decade or so later the book still sold, the letter long forgotten. Allegro had established a reputation. Robin obviously considered getting Allegro on the Hodder list an achievement. It was his initiative which was contributing to the growth of Hodder's reputation in the Sixties when many publishers found the going hard.

Highly intelligent, with an appreciation of literature and music, Robin as editorial director, cared for people more than books or profits.

He was a character. I saw him with odd socks; and once with no socks, interviewing a top author, after being caught in the rain. When I admired his new lightweight suit he claimed he had bought it at the village jumble sale the previous Saturday. As official opener he was first in and spotted the bargain. His office had been refurbished with desk and chairs to match his executive position, but the effect was marred by an ancient harmonium, wheezy and grossly out of place. Between eight forty-five a.m. and nine a.m., as the secretaries arrived, strains of hymn tunes told us he was in.

At his farm I met Sue the ewe. Sue was almost a member of his family. A story circulated that he had taken a manuscript home to read over the weekend and failed to return with it on Monday. Sue the ewe, rumour insisted, had developed a literary taste when the kitchen door was left open.

Robin had exceptional editorial liberty. The chairman and his joint chief-executive, John Attenborough, a former President of the Publishers' Association, both descendants of the founders of the firm, had given him great freedom. The willingness to delegate was a strength of the company.

There was no more genuine admirer of Robin than myself, but I was troubled by what he told me about John Allegro's book. Before the deal was concluded I wished he had shared a synopsis with other scholars. Now there was a commitment to publish.

The finished manuscript went directly from the author to Robin. The normal custom was for a specialist book to be sent to outside readers for professional reactions. The reports would be circulated round the office and considered at an editorial meeting. In the light of these there might be further revision.

In this case I saw no reports. Word circulated that the manuscript's content would be concealed until publication. Press leaks must be avoided. It was an extraordinary book.

The 1970 Spring Catalogue *New Publications* gave it the prime position: a two-page spread included a photograph of Allegro. *The Sacred Mushroom and the Cross* was

> a book that will make every thinking person question what he believes and why . . . His work is a study of the nature and origins of Christianity, within the fertility cults of the ancient Near East. The religion of the Israelites and their successors, the Christians, is now shown to have been founded in a very ancient fertility cult centred on the worship of the sacred mushroom, the red-topped *Amanita Muscaria*.

The sales representatives from their scattered territories arrived for the sales conference in January, 1970, with a heightened sense of expectancy. The grapevine had leaked that this book had enormous sales potential. Representatives, often the best-informed people in publishing, are responsible for getting books into bookshops. They are shrewd. As editors present the titles at a sales conference they take into account the temperament of the presenter and make their own level-headed assessment. If they are not enthused, the bookseller, naturally cautious in what he orders, will sense it. They are discerning, hard-working, well-read.

Robin was the most popular presenter. His word carried weight not only because of his position and academic achievements, but through his honesty and openness. He did not oversell, he did not pretend every book would attract major reviews. He might confess: 'I made an error in taking this, but see what you can do.' When talking of print numbers editors indulge in wishful thinking and double-up; Robin added only ten per cent.

He presented *The Sacred Mushroom and the Cross* with restrained enthusiasm. The salesmen scribbled their notes. When he mentioned the colossal advance payment they knew it was big.

'The serial rights have been sold to the *Sunday Mirror*,' I overheard a few weeks before publication.

'I thought it was a scholarly book.'

'They'll pick up the sensational sections.'

My hope that the book would be overlooked as many titles are dissolved: the *Sunday Mirror* serialisation would be read by millions.

I must get a copy. With the aid of the production department I secured one from the book-binder. It was an impressive production; the price was high for 1970 but the bulk and presentation justified it.

Following my habit I opened the last pages: there were 150 pages of explanatory notes filling a third of the book. Allegro had done some hard labour: there were pages of references to Hebrew/Aramaic: Syriac; Greek, Latin; Arabic/Persian; plus a Biblical index and Sumerian word index.

I turned to the early sections. The New Testament is a 'literary device to spread occult knowledge to the faithful,' I read, 'to tell the story of a rabbi called Jesus, and invest him with the power and names of the major drugs.'

I flipped over the pages. 'The name and titles "John the Baptist" in the New Testament story then, means no more than the "red-topped mushroom" . . .'

About Christ it was blasphemous. Jesus was the prime mushroom symbol. 'In the phallic mushroom, the "man-child" born of the "virgin" womb, we have the reality behind the Christ figure of the New Testament story.' Again, 'Now we face a new revelation in thought which must make us reconsider the validity of the New Testament story. The breakthrough here is not in the field of history but in philology.'

What is philology? The answer was on page three – the science of words, but there was a great deal that remained unexplained. Parts of the book I could not follow but I did understand sufficient to make me ask what this publication was doing on the Hodder and Stoughton list. Surely no scholar, Christian or otherwise, could take it seriously. It would not threaten Christianity: it would discredit the author and the publisher.

The *Sunday Mirror* serial was about to start. While the discerning would laugh it off, for millions of readers the story would be presented as having proved that Christianity was a farce: perverted, misguided, a colourful mushroom.

The serial ran in April. 'A startling theory that Christianity is a hoax based on sex-drug cult,' the heavy, black type read. An illustration of Jesus portrayed him with a mushroom not a cross. It was the combination of religion and sex which sold newspapers.

Michael Green, Principal of the London College of Divinity, and a Hodder author, was shattered to read the extracts and to discover the publisher. His reply was published in the *Sunday Mirror* with the headline, 'A load of old fungus'. He asserted that Allegro had a highly suspect judgment and a bizarre understanding of pagan religions.

Two or three prominent Christians talked of reporting the book to the Director of Public Prosecutions. The *Church of England Newspaper* published the story, and Hodder's publicity manager, an ambitious young Scotsman, spread it round Fleet Street. It was broadcast by the B.B.C. The book had not yet been published, but orders were recorded in bookshops and reservations made in public libraries.

It might have been a publisher's dream. For me it was a nightmare: I was the religious editor. The book was directed head-on against Christ.

Robin wrote a statement to send to those who wrote in protesting following the newspaper serial.

'Very occasionally,' it read, 'perhaps once in a lifetime, a book publisher is offered a work of scholarship which, by the nature of its discoveries, is bound to cause offence . . .'

He went on to explain the author's intention to use his scholar's knowledge of the original Sumerian writing to identify the Hebrew worship of Yahweh-Jehovah with the fertility cults of the ancient civilisations of the Near East. 'He also puts forward a theory, backed by study of the language and practice of these fertility cults, that the Gospels themselves are a myth and that Jesus is a fictional character – not a fact of history.'

Why had Hodder's published? He set out to explain:

'To publish or not to publish' is a question which must have been asked by John Murray in 1859 before he published Darwin's *Origin of Species*. One hundred years later, the Board of Hodder and Stoughton faced the same question and decided on the same positive answer. Without subscribing to John Allegro's more speculative conclusions, we believe that a publisher is concerned with truth, however shocking and explosive it may prove to be. Such a belief is held with particular strength by the Christian publisher who knows that the Christian faith has nothing to fear from the truth which science and scholarship reveal.

It was not a statement which would satisfy those who believed in the deity and Lordship of Jesus Christ. It was nonsense to talk of 'the truth which science and scholarship reveal'.

Christ did not need me to defend him, but to do so is the instinct of his followers. That Allegro was denying my own experience was inconsequential; that he was denying the Son of God in a Hodder publication made me question

67

whether my future was with the firm.

I was isolated. I did not feel free to discuss it with friends outside, and inside that would have been considered disloyal. Whatever the arguments before a book was taken, once a commitment had been made everyone stood behind it. I did not want the members of the church which I attended to know; their esteem for Hodder, with its great religious tradition, would have been rocked.

I tried to tell myself not to get steamed up. Christianity had withstood centuries of onslaught. Would a lecturer from Manchester achieve what Nero had failed to do? And thousands like him?

A press conference was announced for publication day, Monday, May 19th, at three p.m. in St. Paul's House. Allegro would answer questions. I told Robin I would like to participate. I wanted the Christian challenge to the mushroom nonsense to be aired that afternoon.

'No,' he said. 'We're launching Allegro's book. The Christian response can follow.'

The firm had already given me permission to contract the Reverend John King, a former editor of *The Church of England Newspaper*, to write *A Christian View of the Mushroom Myth*, but that would not be out for months. It seemed essential that the religious department of Hodder disassociated themselves from Allegro on publication day.

Robin left my office and I looked through the window at the dome of St. Paul's Cathedral with its cross. Thousands had gazed at it in the blitz as I did now. I had behind my desk a photograph taken in the full fury of a raid, the sky lit by incendiaries, the buildings all around blazing uncontrollably, the cross a cherished symbol.

For me this was a blitz. The explosive had not been dropped by an enemy but by Robin, who had taught me all I knew about publishing and much more. It had not been unleashed by an unbeliever: he was a licensed reader in the Anglican church. His book, *Partly Living*, published three years earlier, had suggested the way forward in the spiritual life was to recognise the marks on the trees left by previous travellers. He had included a section on a favourite topic – death. 'What a fantastic future opens out for us,' he wrote, 'and Christianity insists that it will indeed be ours, just as it is a present state for countless millions now – the millions who have died in the Lord.'

Albert Schweitzer, who founded the famous hospital at Lambarene, once created a furore with his writing on Jesus. When asked if he called himself a Christian he said: 'There are two sorts of Christians – the dogmatic and the undogmatic. I am the undogmatic.'

Robin was undogmatic. It was the difference between us.

As publication day drew near I considered resignation. It was not a daytime thought. It surfaced nightly between three-thirty a.m. and four-thirty a.m. when I sat up in bed and faced the questions.

Was I concerned with my own reputation? With the reputation of Hodder? With the Name of Christ?

Would resignation be honourable?

Or simply spectacular?

'Allegro isn't worth it,' I told myself, seeing him, in Shakespeare's words, as a 'poor player that struts and frets his hour upon the stage, then is heard no more'.

'But the faith is,' I argued back.

Soon after five I would fall asleep, the question unanswered.

'Publish for the committed,' Leonard Cutts had said. But how committed should the publisher be? This was my problem with Allegro. I could not as religious editor, as a Christian believer, stand aside as a disinterested spectator. All that I believed was involved.

I would not resign. By doing so I would magnify the issue, accord Allegro further importance. By resigning I would maximise the damage to the company's Christian heritage.

I would make a public protest.

'It may damage your chances of getting on the Hodder Board where you can be more influential in preventing such publications,' a friend objected. Hints had been made over the previous year that a Board appointment might not be too distant. Boardrooms are the place of decision: I wanted to be there.

I was confused, uncertain of my motives, but the conviction grew that I must disassociate my department from the book whatever the consequences.

69

On publication day, as the secretaries, seeking the sun, went out to lunch, I sat in my office and summoned up my courage. It would have been easy to take the afternoon off, to watch the ducks in St. James Park, or to go home and mow the lawns, and forget the press conference, but I could not abdicate what I saw as my responsibility.

I made my way to Robin's office.

'If I can't speak to the press directly,' I said, 'may I suggest a compromise. I would like to distribute a written statement to the journalists.'

'If you really must,' he said, after a long pause, 'but I'd prefer you didn't, obviously.'

'Thanks, Robin. I'll write something and make copies.'

I forgot lunch and typed out my declaration for the journalists. I did not think the book should be banned, as some had suggested; it was nonsense to refer it to the Director of Public Prosecutions; but I regretted the publication by Hodder and Stoughton and the pretence, as I saw it, that here was a major breakthrough.

I am sorry that Hodder have published this book, although I know they did so believing it to be a genuine scholarly contribution by a celebrated author. I understand the Board considered it at length and approve their decision not to be afraid of manuscripts which might be shocking or explosive, but before reaching their decision to publish this book they should have consulted a representative selection of other scholars . . . I do not like censorship and in a company this size no one employee approves of every title. Nevertheless I believe this book will prove *unnecessarily* offensive to many people . . .

Hodder and Stoughton have backed the Christian faith for more than a hundred years, and have published many quality books knowing there would be little or no profit. Its contribution to Christian belief has been magnificent, probably unequalled by any other British publisher, which makes the publication of this book, marked by speculation and false deductions, all the more sad.

I concluded: 'I am grateful to the Directors of Hodder and Stoughton for permission to distribute this statement.'

There was forty-five minutes before the press conference. I slipped into St. Paul's Cathedral and recalled my visit there on my first day at Hodder, four years before, and my commission: 'Do not limit your Christian publishing by your own experience. Publish for the whole church of Jesus Christ. For all men who truly believe that Jesus Christ is the Son of God.'

The boardroom was thronged with journalists. The quality papers, the popular press, the overseas correspondents, the news-agencies, were all represented. John Allegro, a handsome man in his early forties, took his seat alongside Robin. In front of them were two bowls of mushrooms – our publicity manager never missed a chance – and a pile of my typed statements.

It was pitched low-key. Allegro described his book as an attempt to 'clear the decks' for new thinking. There were questions and answers, in good humour, but the journalists were uncomprehending when he moved from the mushroom as a symbol of sex and religion to talk about his philological borrowings. Each reporter took a copy of my statement as he left and because the story of conflict within Hodder was easier to understand than philology it stole the headlines.

Rita Marshall in *The Times* quoted me at length under the heading *Firm to publish answer to mushroom book*. At the end of her story there was a reference to what the author had said, to the critical letters he had received from people who said they were going to pray for him.

A week after publication it remained news in *The Times*. Professor Sir Godfrey Driver and fourteen other scholars published a letter stating that in their view the book was not based on any philological or other evidence which they could regard as scholarly.

The reviewers elsewhere gave the author a rough ride. In vain he must have looked for intelligent support. Dr. Henry Chadwick, Dean of Christ Church, Oxford, wrote in the *Daily Telegraph*: 'Mr. Allegro's reputation as a man of judgment and learning, already widely questioned, is likely to be shattered by this curious publication.' He concluded: 'Perhaps there may be some sad minds to whom this book offers a liberating experience. But three guineas' worth of

71

*Amanita muscaria* would be better value.'

'Mr. Allegro sometimes talks about Greek, and about this he talks such nonsense that it seems unsafe to take him seriously even as a philologist,' said the *Sunday Times* reviewer. He reached the conclusion that the author 'is hardly to be taken seriously on his own ground, and not at all when he leaves it. He appears to be obsessed with a subject which has wasted years of his talents.'

The *Church Times* believed that 'any investigator who comes up with these conclusions can hardly be expected to be taken seriously'; the *Catholic Herald* spoke of the high proportion of speculative Sumerian verbal forms; while the *Baptist Times* reviewer declared: 'This is the most fantastic and misleading book I have ever been asked to review.'

Robin stood by the author. Allegro needed friends. If a responsible editor launches a book he does not desert the writer when the flak falls, and whatever Robin's private thoughts, he spoke in generous terms of Allegro. He could have hidden behind the fact that he commissioned the book without knowing how speculative its conclusions would be. He chose not to do so.

For a few weeks the book prospered, and then sales slowed abruptly. Later the same year, Hodder published *A Christian View of the Mushroom Myth*. It was written with creditable speed, and a typical reviewer found it 'an entertaining, hard-hitting and intensely readable indictment of the Allegro myth', but sales were modest. No one anymore was concerned with mushrooms. Except for eating.

Another publisher offered me a post 'at whatever your present salary is, plus a bonus'.

'I'm staying with Hodder, if they'll have me,' I replied. 'It's a great firm that's made an error.'

When John Attenborough wrote his history of Hodder I turned to see if Allegro scored a mention. He did. 'If Denniston made publishing mistakes,' he wrote, 'for instance with John Allegro's *The Sacred Mushroom and the Cross* (1970) which called into question the language and the truth of the New Testament and lost the firm some good friends . . . they were part of his shock tactics for which the Board shared full responsibility.'

No editor with a major list can look back without confessing there was some book he should not have published, but it was regrettable that Robin's should have attempted to blast the foundations upon which the faith, our nation, and this publishing house were built. It harmed Allegro, I regret to say. It did not harm the Gospel.

Was I justified in protesting? Would I do it again? Did I accomplish anything? The reader must supply his own answers. I do not think I could have stayed with the company and built up the religious publishing list over the next decade if I had failed to make my protest.

On April 1st, the following year, as a direct result of Robin's recommendation, I was appointed a director of Hodder and Stoughton, and given control of what was and what was not published in the religious field. No other director would be involved. The decisions would be mine alone. It was a privilege few companies would have given to an editor after five years. Robin sent a handwritten note:

I am delighted that you have joined the Board of Hodder and Stoughton. It is a wonderful firm to be in, and wonderful to have you work in it. It's easy in day to day stress to forget our good fortune in being where we are, but if we were anywhere else we'd be very aware of the pleasures of St. Paul's House . . .

I am sure that you and I are a good partnership. We understand, and speaking personally like each other – the best basis for any partnership. More strength to your elbow. With very best congratulations.

I agreed wholeheartedly with his definition of a good partnership: not agreement but understanding and liking each other. He was the finest and most sympathetic boss I ever had.

# 9

# THE LIFE-BLOOD

Dr. Samuel Johnson, when he had compiled his dictionary, wrote in the preface of being faint with weariness under a task which had proved as tough as the labours of the anvil and the mine. Because writing is exacting, calling for stamina, energy, willpower and talent, a publisher must provide unremitting encouragement, admiring the writer and the writing.

I was invited to give a lecture to fifty religious publishers from Third World countries. 'Love God,' I told them. 'If you don't, move to another area of publishing.' They scribbled it down in their notebooks. 'Love your books,' I went on, 'or you'll never succeed with them.' I spoke slowly for a few had difficulty with English. 'Love your authors,' I concluded. 'If you can't, stop publishing for them.'

To love one's authors was not an original thought. It was underlined for me in an article in *The Bookseller* by Anthony Blond, a London publisher. He wrote:

Like vintage cars and indoor plants, authors must be treated with love and care if they are to be kept. When an author leaves a publisher the cry is that he was not loved enough. This may mean the publisher did not watch his television play last Tuesday, or is devoting too much time to a shiny new author. A conscientious publisher may find himself becoming a nanny, banker, doctor, and travel agent to the author. This may mean the loan of a fiver, or housing for a few days an aged and incontinent red setter.

I have acted as banker and travel agent and, although I

have not been asked to take in a red setter, I did find an author on the doorstep one Saturday night with an armful of dirty washing. 'Could I borrow your washing-machine?' she gasped.

More significant than caring for a red setter is encouragement. The hesitant author of a first book and the famous writer cry for it. I recall an established novelist losing faith in her new book at the halfway stage. 'I can't continue,' she wrote. 'The dialogue's wrong, the plot's not working out.' It was a distress signal. A senior fiction editor cancelled his engagements and caught a train to spend, not an hour, but two days with her. On the first day they barely mentioned the incomplete manuscript on her desk. They trekked in the hills, drinking in the fresh air, she glad to be away from the blank pages which had to be filled for reviewers to praise and her public to buy.

A year later another publisher offered that author a substantial sum to leave Hodder. Nothing would make her break the link.

'Authors are the life-blood of publishing,' our chairman would remind us.

It took me time to discover that success did not diminish the desire, not for honeyed words, but for honest appreciation. I wrote to a distinguished author whose books had sold millions of copies, to congratulate him on the quality of the typescript he had submitted.

'Come to lunch,' he wrote back. As we sat over coffee he said, 'Your letter helped. My self-confidence was at a low ebb.'

I looked in astonished incredulity. His manner was too serious for me to laugh.

'You don't need anyone to say you're good,' I protested. 'Look at the reviews, your sales, your royalties.'

His wife refilled my cup.

'Edward, I've a marvellous wife.' It was an understatement. 'She's my best helper. She types all the manuscripts. In a thousand ways she spoils me: in one way she disappoints. When I give her something to type I want to hear her commendation. She never says anything. Not in twenty years. Perfect typing when I want her praise, to hear her say, "It's great!"'

She smiled. 'It's true. I'm not competent to judge.'

Big sales, quotable reviews, but he longs to hear from those he loves and from those who publish, 'It's great'.

However mechanised and computerised publishing might become writing is a lonely, personal assignment. 'It starts,' one Scots theologian said, 'with applying the seat of the pants to the seat of the chair.'

'There are always so many distractions like toothache and indigestion,' Beverley Nichols told Winston Churchill. 'You've got to get over that,' Churchill told him, recommending that he should go to his room every morning at nine o'clock and write for four hours. 'If you sit waiting for inspiration, you will sit waiting until you are an old man. Writing is like any other job – like marching any army, for instance. If you sit down and wait until the weather is fine, you won't get very far with your troops. Kick yourself, irritate yourself; but *write*; it's the only way.'

Good writing is not dependent on congenial surroundings, however welcome, a comfortable chair, a desk, a typewriter, a pleasant outlook. In the Middle Ages the cloisters were the workshop of the scribes and on winter days when the wind howled their fingers were numbed by the cold. One monk wrote upon his manuscript: 'The book which you now see was written in the outer seats of the cloister. When I wrote I froze; and what I could not write by the beams of day I finished by candlelight.'

The Apostle Paul wrote in prison. So did John Bunyan. Some of the most creative modern writing has come from Soviet prison camps.

'In *Puritan's Progress*, Monica Furlong describes Bunyan using up the interminable hours, shutting out the lamentations and cursing, the aimless chatter and the mindless rambling of his fellow prisoners, as he wrote *The Pilgrim's Progress*.

Bunyan had entered prison as a comparatively young man and came out as a middle-aged one. He had changed none of his original beliefs, nor had he bowed to persecution; there is however, a richness of humanity in *The Pilgrim's Progress* which seems to owe much to his suffering. He had entered prison as a man of unusual imagination, of natural verbal gifts and of genuine talent as a preacher. He left it as a literary genius.

Memorable writing can be born in situations of intense suffering. William Cowper wrote *The Task* between bouts of mental illness.

> I was a stricken deer, that left the herd
> Long since; with many an arrow deep infixt,
> My panting side was charg'd, when I withdrew
> To seek a tranquil death in distant shades.
> There was I found by one who had himself
> Been hurt by th'archers. In his side he bore,
> And in his hands and feet, the cruel scars.

I think of two authors whose devotional writing has inspired thousands. Both have known severe depression, one needed treatment in a psychiatric hospital, the other has been periodically suicidal. Out of their darkness has come choice writing which makes compulsory reading. Dr. W. E. Sangster, the British Methodist leader, whose books circulated throughout the English-speaking world, constructed three books during his final painful illness. *Give God a Chance* consisted of '100 Basic Religious Questions Plainly Answered'. The remaining two books were *Westminster Sermons*, Volumes One and Two. They appeared after his death.

There are writers who turn an apparent handicap to advantage. Among these was William Barclay. I went to see him for a mid-afternoon appointment at Glasgow University, where he was Professor of Divinity and Biblical Criticism. I knocked on his study door. There was no reply. I could hear him typing from inside so I knocked again. An undergraduate came along the corridor and told me to go in. 'He's deaf,' he said. 'He'll have turned off his hearing aid.' I opened the door, he saw me and switched on.

In his autobiography *Testament of Faith*, published by Mowbrays, he speaks of the positive advantages of his deafness.

It means that it is possible to sleep anywhere – even in a railway station. And – most useful of all – it means that you need only listen when you want to. If the speaker is boring, then it is the easiest thing in the world to switch him off! I can retire into a world of my own whenever I want to . . . Of course, I would like not to be deaf, but I have never found that being deaf has stopped me doing anything I wanted to do.'

His friend, Denis Duncan, wrote:

When he is at work in the study off comes the hearing aid, and he can hear nothing! The phone rings in vain. The doorbell goes unanswered. William Barclay is in the world of silence where concentration is complete and creative work is at its maximum. At eleven p.m. he falls asleep but only for an hour. At midnight he is awake again and works till two a.m.'

When he died I asked R. D. Kernohan to edit some tributes to this scholar and author who wrote nearly seventy books. Hodder published it with the title, *William Barclay, the Plain Uncommon Man*. It included the story of a fellow professor's remarks when he was missing for forty-five minutes in a mid-morning break; 'He's probably just used the time to write another book.'

The most costly book in my experience was *Out of Silence* by Mary Sorrell, published in 1969. It took the author years of laborious, painful, determined effort.

Mary lived in London's West End. She was a broadcaster, writer and painter. On Christmas Day, 1954, she had a cerebal haemorrhage which deprived her of speech. She could neither read nor write. Words lost their meaning for her. Her wheeling brain never ceased wheeling. The effort of trying to find a word or utter a syllable was unbelievably exhausting. When the hospital trolley came round with breakfast she could only point out what she wanted.

One day she opened a hospital New Testament at random. She made out a word here and there. It was such terribly hard work and seemed to hurt her brain more than anything else. Yet something made her try to write out a few words. She would then lie back completely spent.

She began to collect words either from hearing or reading them. She kept them in her home-made personal Word Book. They were in no specific order so she had to glance down the endless columns until she found the one she was seeking. With the help of lexicons, *Roget's Thesaurus* and the *Oxford Dictionary* she learned to read and write and speak again. It took years.

The moment came when she opened her typewriter just in case. She laid her fingertips on the keys and very slowly typed her name, MARY SORRELL, tears of gratitude streaming down her cheeks. Then haltingly, and with endless mistakes, she typed her address.

She became a committed Christian after her kind lady doctor took her one Sunday to All Souls, just off Oxford Street, to hear the Rector. As she listened to the sermon, his interpretation of the words of Jesus were what she had unknowingly been seeking: Jesus said, 'Come unto me, and I will give you rest.' In a split second she gave herself wholeheartedly to him.

Now as a Christian she wanted to share her faith through her pen, but even thinking was a torment. Often her brain could scarcely follow the services which she attended. To write a short story took months; to write a book would take years, but she made a start.

Her consultant physician, the Rector, and many friends provided comfort and stimulus. She wrote:

I made endless mistakes and continually lost my way. My damaged brain seemed to enjoy throwing dust into my eyes, but laughter, that precious gift from God, came to my aid . . . My brain seems to crawl over the surface of the paper, and my hand follows. My ear however is a reasonably good guide. Before assembling many of the sentences I have just had to try them out to hear if their rhythmical sound is correct. By that sound, even when the words are not actually musical, I can always tell whether a phrase is good or not. Yet I cannot always be sure that any sentence is correct because my grammar so often lets me down.

It took years to reach the twentieth, the final chapter. There had been constant breaks because of physical setbacks and hospital treatment. For eighteen months she did not write. She repeatedly thought of tearing it all and her Word Book into little pieces. 'The grey wastes of space close in on my brain, and like ragged clouds they are often laden with sorrows. My Word Book is ever beside me, yet sometimes when I feverishly turn the pages they look full of nothing but emptiness.'

The last paragraph of her book acknowledged God in whose inexplicable care she had triumphed over sadness and heartbreak.

In the beginning of the first half of this book I recalled then only a pale recollection of his goodness to me; yet unhesitatingly I yielded to his outstretched hands and silently accepted his love. And shining through the darkness of that night in the ward when I was able to murmur just two words – 'Our Father' – I now hear his soundless voice breathing in my ear, 'I am the Good Shepherd; the Good Shepherd giveth his life for the sheep. My sheep hear my voice, and I know them and they follow me.'

A friend of Mary's sent the typescript to Elizabeth Goudge, the novelist, whose books had graced the Hodder list for more than twenty-five years. 'This book,' Miss Goudge wrote, 'has been written at great cost, not to bring relief to the writer, but with hope that it may bring encouragement to those who are fighting a battle that may be not unlike her own.'

I handled the pages, living through the physical and spiritual torment with her, marvelling at the creative impulse, seeing her expanding sentences from single words until she brought them to a state of near perfection. I knew Hodder would publish regardless of profitability. Soon I sensed the book would need no special pleading. On its merit it would justify itself in the market place.

Mary Sorrell kept watch on her letterbox. 'It has practically become human to me. It is the most provocative object I have because it can be coy, sinister, forlorn and delighted.' Our letter of acceptance almost took her breath away.

Before she died, some eighteen months later, I was able to tell her of a second printing. We spoke on the telephone and she confided that cancer had been diagnosed, but my memory is of her laughter. 'God's in his heaven,' the words came slowly, 'all's right with the world.'

*Out of Silence* is now out of print but whenever I see a copy on my shelves I am reminded of her courage and dogged perseverance.

Windy cloisters, prison sentences and ill-health are no deterrent to the writer: nor is age. After John Attenborough retired from being joint chief executive of Hodder, he wrote first a history of the firm and then, at seventy, a first novel, *One Man's Inheritance*. The critics liked it and so did the public: within months it had to be reprinted. The paperback and the American rights were sold.

Special among the authors in their seventies and eighties with whom I worked was Catherine Bramwell Booth, grand-daughter of the founder of The Salvation Army, General William Booth. In February 1970, I received a handwritten note from her.

Next Tuesday 17th we hope to see you at our family luncheon party. If you could be here about 12.30 there would be time for introductions before the meal. I am so pleased you are able to come.

The occasion was unique. It was a reunion of the remaining members of the family which, with unflagging faith, had started and in succeeding generations established The Salvation Army worldwide. Commissioner Booth, at eighty-seven, was publishing her biography, *Catherine Booth*, the story of the mother of the Salvation Army. At the celebration lunch were the author's sisters, Doris, Olive and Mary. Olive, in particular, had spent her retirement checking and ordering references and in the drudgery of typing. Apart from myself, representing Hodder, there were no non-family guests.

The retired Commissioner greeted me at the door, upright, alert, magnificent in her old-style uniform. While she took my coat she left me standing in the hall by a bust of her father, General Bramwell Booth, and a large drum with furled flag and framed motto, 'As for me and my house we will serve the LORD'. She called it the Little Corner.

In the dining-room she was evidently the commanding officer. We sat around the oval-shaped table, a present from the founder and his wife to her mother. The walls were covered with photographs and paintings of the family.

The author was born in 1883, entering The Salvation Army in 1903. She was appointed International Secretary for the Salvation Army in Europe in 1917, and was put in command of the Women's Social Work in Great Britain and Ireland in 1926. She was International Secretary for Europe from 1946 to 1948.

Over lunch she recalled my first visit to North Court. I had heard that she had written a biography of Catherine Booth which no one would publish because of its length: 1,200 pages. It had been rejected by Hodder before my arrival as being too long to make commercial publishing sense. It was the kind of manuscript one weighed rather than read. She packed it in a Salvation Army bonnet-box for me to take away.

Whatever the previous decision I was sure the Hodder Board would support me. Having met the Commissioner I was under her spell. She had started to write the book in earnest in 1949, but put it aside as their mother was with them. 'I didn't want to rob us of our time together.' Mother died at ninety-six. In 1957 she took up the book again.

When the meal was finished we moved to the comfortable lounge with its coffee cups and Salvation Army hymn-books and assortment of tables, chairs and sofas. For an hour, accompanied on an organ dating back to the beginning of the century, we sang the hymns written by the Booth family.

*Catherine Booth* is among the most satisfying religious biographies ever published. *The Times* devoted a major feature article to the book and its author. A South African reviewer said:

This is a mammoth memoir, packed with interest . . . It is much more than a biography of a beloved grandmother;

it is a history of her times – 1829 to 1890 – and a revealing account of the advance of the Salvation Army throughout those years. It is also a most poignant love story: for William Booth and Catherine, throughout their life together, were passionately, sincerely and deeply in love, and united in their love to the service of God.

In 1978 the *Sunday Times* noted that at ninety-four the Commissioner had been voted, to her great amusement, 'Best Speaker of the Year' by the Guild of Professional Toastmasters; that she had appeared three times on television, broadcast twice on radio *and started writing her fifth book*.

As I write she is ninety-six and busily recording her spiritual experiences.

A prison sentence, a physical handicap, a terminal illness, the frailties of old age: none of these are adequate excuse for an author with something to say, with a story worth the telling. As Commissioner Bramwell Booth says, 'I feel I ought to do it and the feeling becomes so heavy that I have to.'

While ever that urge remains the life-blood of publishers will continue to flow.

# 10

# ANOTHER LIFE?

Death was a reality I barely recognised in the first half of my life. I thought about it in publishing terms when a successful London businessman, who had recently lost his wife, called and persuaded me that we should commission a book on what Christians believed about life after death. He offered to pay for advertisements to make the proposed book known in newspapers like *The Times* and the *Daily Telegraph*.

The outcome of his visit to our office was *Hereafter*, written by David Winter, a B.B.C. producer, with the sub-title 'A new look at an old question: What happens after death?' One reviewer described it as 'A clear scholarly spiritual exposition of orthodox Christian belief,' while the *Church Times* said, 'It could well be put into the hands of many whose personal situation, such as the experience of a serious illness, is causing them to think about the ultimate questions perhaps for the first time.'

The book evoked an immediate and warm response. David Winter had expected that any letters would have been from elderly people, but there were plenty from young people, from student age upwards. The most moving letters came from those who had been bereaved. One woman in particular, who described herself as having a more than academic interest in the subject, 'being in her eighties', wrote to say that through reading the book she was now, for the first time in her life, able to believe that life does not end at death, and that her new-found faith had brought her great joy and comfort.

In a reprint of the book, the author told how one woman wrote to tell him what happened as she was going through the personal papers of her mother, who had died a few days before.

> Suddenly she was overcome with grief and with doubt about the Christian doctrine of the resurrection of the dead [she and her mother were Roman Catholics]· She began to cry, and the tears fell on the papers in front of her. She picked up the papers to move them, and found that on the top of the pile was a copy of *Hereafter*, which her mother had obviously been reading. It was, as she said, like a personal message of comfort.

For me, the subject was to assume more than an academic interest. Questions about personal and human destiny were to become critical. I had never seen anyone die, although as a young reporter I had seen lifeless bodies, but soon I would want to be assured that life hereafter was not just wishful thinking but a bright light of hope based on a solid foundation.

My serious thinking started when Gwen's mother was admitted to St. Christopher's Hospice, situated in a tree-lined road in South London. She had undergone several operations for cancer and was now a terminal patient. There was nothing more the surgeons could do.

Her last three weeks at home had been distressing, with a call for pain-killing drugs every few hours, day and night, and she was in some agony when admitted to the Hospice. Within hours there was a transformation. When Gwen and I called in the evening she was propped up in bed in a gay bed-jacket looking better than we had seen her in months. She gave us a list of the items we were to bring for the toys she planned to make.

The Hospice, founded by Dr. Cecily Saunders, had fifty-four beds in small wards. It was a registered charity, not a state hospital, although the National Health Service made a contribution towards running costs.

We asked about the change in Gwen's mother. The ward sister, shortly leaving to be a missionary in Africa, explained that Dr. Saunders did not permit pain to dominate the consciousness of patients. She prescribed drugs in such a way that it was possible to control the level of pain and to bring about complete relaxation. The fear of recurring pain was banished. 'Divine is the work to subdue pain,' said Hippocrates in the fourth century BC, and we witnessed it for ourselves.

We returned the next day with a basket of shopping; tiny dolls to be dressed; material for making items for a local sale of work; writing paper and envelopes. In the next bed a frail lady, with days to live, was completing a water-colour painting.

'Will I ever go home again?' It was the question we had feared, but she was matter-of-fact, wanting a frank, not evasive answer.

'Probably not, Mother.' Gwen put her arms around her. 'But you know where you're going.'

'Yes,' she smiled. 'I've a lot to do first. Like sorting out my affairs.'

'I'll make a list of the things we should talk about.'

From that day her death was assumed rather than mentioned. It was an open secret: we were all party to it.

'Will I suffer at the end?' she asked once, but was reassured not by our words but by observing others who died peacefully as if in a deep sleep. Between January and May twelve patients died in the small ward of eight beds, but in place of distress we witnessed in their last days a quality of life, quiet acceptance, courage and even laughter.

She wanted to say goodbye to our boisterous West Highland white terrier, and permission was given for her to be brought, wagging her tail, into the ward. She was a bonus for all the patients.

In those hours sitting by her bed I had ample time to think and to observe how patients and relatives faced approaching death. A few never accepted the fact, coping by resorting to make-believe. One woman talked of her holiday plans to the end. She believed death happened to others.

Unlike some hospitals, the Hospice did not encourage evasion of the subject, which can lead to greater distress, but there was no brooding.

'In my experience,' said Dr. Saunders, 'I find that the truth dawns gradually on many, even most, of the dying even when they do not ask and are not told. They accept it quietly and often gratefully but some may not wish to discuss it and we must respect their reticence.'

Astonishingly little has been written on how Christian believers have faced up to the knowledge of their imminent departure from this world. Dr. W. E. Sangster, the Methodist preacher, most of whose books were published by Hodder, made some notes, when he knew he would not preach again. He wrote:

Yet I would like you to know that God has never been nearer to me than now. I have had much grace never to murmur. At no period of my life have I had so much time for prayer and, perhaps, part of my pain in not being able to preach is the knowledge that I have deeper things to say than I ever had. Infinite wisdom and infinite love are at work for me, and a man who is sure of that can endure anything.

In *Doctor Sangster*, a biography by his son Paul, we read of what that endurance included. He had progressive muscular atrophy. At first he was able to walk with two sticks and considerable help, but eventually became increasingly incapacitated so that only his right arm and hand were of serious use to him. His voice entirely vanished and swallowing became difficult.

His faith held. He shrank from company because he did not care for the undisguised surprise of visitors at the physical change in him. He wrote:

But *is* this personality change?
I was never quieter within.
I was never more serene and unhurried.
I was never more sure of God.
I was never more grateful for mercies.

Never more sure of God. It was how we felt on the Sunday before Gwen's mother died. The Anglican chaplain, never far away, invited us to join in a brief service of Holy Communion around her bed. Sensing it would be our last together we had to keep tight control on our emotions

87

but we experienced the peace of God.

She continued with her doll-dressing until Tuesday morning. On Thursday night she died.

We were thankful for the love and care she had received in this famous Hospice, for the alleviation of the physical discomforts of her illness, for the vision of Dr. Saunders.

The Hospice showed continued interest in patients' relatives. We learned that on the first anniversary of a death they sent a message expressing concern for their welfare. I little realised that in twelve months, when that communication arrived, I would have faced the biggest crisis in my life.

Daily visiting over the winter months, a turmoil of emotions, and a sense of loss, had left Gwen exhausted. From the day of the funeral her energy evaporated. She gave up the job she had done on three mornings a week, she found the housework a burden. I took her on holiday to the Lake District, where we stayed in a favoured hotel overlooking Derwentwater. We took gentle short journeys in the day to villages like Grasmere, where William Wordsworth lived in Dove Cottage for fourteen years, and we motored home across the Yorkshire Dales; but it was an effort.

The pace of our lives had to slow in the following months, more time at home, fewer outside activities. We bought a colour television set. Reading by the fireside together, instead of entertaining friends, became the pattern as the evenings became darker.

Gwen re-read her favourite novelists: D. E. Stevenson and Elizabeth Goudge. She had edited *The Elizabeth Goudge Christmas Book* and felt safe with both authors.

'There's not enough action in them,' I told her thinking in particular of Elizabeth Goudge.

'That's why they appeal,' she said. 'I don't want drama.'

At Christmas, Michael Attenborough, who had taken Robin Denniston's place at Hodder, told me to take extra holiday to help with the shopping. I asked our Christmas guests not to come. Gwen had never before been depressed but now the doctor prescribed anti-depressants. 'It happens sometimes when a close relative dies,' he said.

In the New Year she developed a severe cough; on the coldest night of the year she awoke with chest pains. 'Dear Jesus, please help me,' she cried, as I held her. Next morning on icy roads, worse than any for ten years, I hurried to the doctor for consultation unknown to her. He was reassuring. 'Give her time,' he said.

Hodder published medical books and in my lunch hour I turned to them to find an answer. It is not a pursuit I recommend. My anxiety increased.

In the early hours of Tuesday, March 16th, I assisted her downstairs; breathing was easier when she was propped in a chair.

'Go back to bed,' she urged. 'You must sleep if you're going to work. I'll call you when breakfast's ready.'

Eventually, I went upstairs, not closing my eyes, listening for her. Her cough was frightening. After one bout I put on my dressing-gown and went to fetch her a drink.

We huddled by the big electric fire gazing at each other, wondering what the future held. I recalled the early days of our marriage, going without luxuries for two years to save the deposit for a house, then the joy of moving into our own place. I thought of her happy encounter with the Wycliffe Bible Translators, of her five years in their British office, of the children of a missionary family who spent Christmas holidays with us.

As the light of the cold March day began to break she asked to look through the window. I drew the curtain and put my arm around her. She started to cough again and moments later collapsed on the floor. I summoned our caring next door neighbour who was round in seconds and telephoned for the doctor. He came quickly, but Gwen was already unconscious. He gave her an injection: almost as he did so she died. She was forty-eight.

It is odd what you think of at such a moment. The previous Thursday she had wanted to deny herself a small luxury. 'It's an extravagance,' she said, thinking of the cost. All her life she had been reluctant to spend on herself. I had insisted on the purchase. 'I'm glad I did,' was my first thought.

The doctor put a friendly hand on my shoulder. 'I can't believe it,' he said. He packed his black bag. There was nothing more a medical man could do. 'There'll have to be a post-mortem.'

Gwen dead? I could not believe it. Yes, with my eyes, but not with my heart. We had built a life together, and planned a future and now, without a goodbye, she was gone. Was it really the end? Or a momentous step for her to a new life in a new environment?

Neighbours and friends called. When I showed them in I was reasonably composed, but between their visits I walked round the house unable to accept. 'Gwen, don't leave me, I need you.'

How much I was to discover. I thought I would be brave and I was not. I thought I could stand on my own feet, alone, and I could not. Friends said I coped marvellously: they were wrong. I had joined, for the first time, the fellowship of those who suffered.

I went to the shops, not to make a purchase, but to see normal life going on outside. The world had not stopped. Only my world. When I came back to the house an hour later her spirit still lingered. Her presence was real. I wanted to hold on to her, but as I stood by where she had died I knew I must release her.

'Darling,' I said softly, 'go now. I want you to be well again.'

The house was suddenly empty.

A little later the doctor telephoned. 'Your wife had cancer,' he said. 'Lung cancer.'

Bedtime came and I went uptstairs with five or six books under my arm to see me through the night. I fell asleep and awoke after two hours. I picked up each book in turn but the words blurred. There were hundreds of volumes in the house but not one for that night. I took *A Book of Comfort* by Elizabeth Goudge, and read the lines of Brother Lawrence, John Milton, William Cowper, Robert Browning, St. Francis of Assisi, but my heart was stilled by more ancient words spoken by Isaiah.

He giveth power to the faint; and to him that hath no might he increaseth strength.
Even the youths shall faint and be weary, and the young men shall utterly fall;

90

But they that wait upon the Lord shall renew their strength; they shall mount up with wings as eagles; they shall run and not be weary; they shall walk, and not faint . . .
Sing, O heavens, and be joyful, O earth; and break forth into singing, O mountains; for the Lord hath comforted his people, and will have compassion upon his afflicted.

My family were in the North of England, so I leaned heavily on friends, telephoning them in dark moments at unsociable hours. On Sunday morning I tuned in to a B.B.C. broadcast from a Methodist church and I found myself singing, 'Oh love that will not let me go, I rest my weary soul on thee'. I found a recording and played it when my spirits dropped.

Did I believe there was another life? I clipped an article from *The Telegraph* Colour Supplement by Roy Bolitho, a Cornish writer, whose wife had died of cancer. He had not been an especially religious person, but he had found there was a basic need for human beings to believe in immortality. 'The idea of immortality is the strongest lifeline to the grief-stricken. Everything that sustains this belief will sustain the person.'

He suggested, therefore, that it was better to give a bereaved person plants that reflower rather than cut flowers, so that the continuance of life, and not its brief blossoming, was suggested.

But was the belief in immortality no more than wishful thinking, no more than a concept to help us cope, to make the loss bearable? Was there a basis for such faith or were we indulging in fantasy?

I recalled what I had believed when Gwen lived – the untested faith. It was a conviction based on Christ's resurrection from the dead, that he was seen by many after his resurrection. The resurrection is the cornerstone of faith in immortality. If Christ is dead, there is no hope and 'those who have fallen asleep in Christ have perished'. Without the resurrection of Christ thoughts of immortality are at best hopeful speculation.

The disciples believed in the bodily resurrection of Christ. Peter, in the first Christian sermon, declared that

Jesus, whom the Jews had crucified, God had raised from the dead and exalted him to heaven where he was seated at God's right hand. Paul believed in Christ's resurrection. He told us that the resurrected Saviour appeared to more than 500 brethren at one time. 'Then he appeared to James, then to all the apostles. Last of all, as to one untimely born, he appeared also to me' (1 Cor. 15. 3–8).

At the funeral service I asked the vicar if we might sing, 'O love that will not let me go'. Surrounded by friends, and Christian assurance it was not difficult to believe, but the following Sunday morning in church, sitting alone, the tears ran uncontrollably, and I needed to know at a new level whether because he lived she would live also.

The tears would not stop. I could not escape from the pew, one end blocked by a pillar, the other by two worshippers. Nor could I run away from her absence. I do not know what the vicar said but there came a fresh certainty that all who are in Christ shall be made alive. 'But each in his own order; Christ the first fruits, then at his coming those who belong to Christ' (1 Cor. 15: 23). We would be re-united. There would be no deformity, no evidence of cancer, no physical weakness for our lowly bodies would be changed 'to be like his glorious body' (Phil. 3: 21).

Through the tears faith held.

Hodder colleagues, like Tony and Jane Collins, became as close as family and the firm became a substitute for home. Paul Hodder-Williams and John Attenborough had retired, and Robin Denniston had moved to another publishers, but support came from all of them; and from their successors, Philip Attenborough, Hodder's present chairman, his brother Michael, and Eric Major.

Hodder had moved their main office from St. Paul's House to extensive purpose-built premises near Sevenoaks, Kent. Dr. Donald Coggan, Archbishop of Canterbury, had agreed to open them in April and I was invited to chauffeur him and his wife, Jean, from the railway station. I did not share my sorrow with him, but Philip Attenborough must have told them, for that night the Archbishop sent a hand-written letter from Lambeth Palace. Like every letter, regardless of source, it brought warmth and solace.

I was to give a lecture to a Christian booksellers and

publishers conference in Bristol and had started to prepare it on the Sunday before Gwen's death, quoting some words of William Temple which she had written out for me.

The causes of health, as the causes of sickness are very many, but among the forces which will tend to keep us in health will be a faith which is extended to a real expectation of God's goodness in every department of our life.

Gwen had lived in the expectation of God's goodness. God's goodness, I believed, was evident in the manner of her death, in the fashion in which he answered her prayer, 'Dear Jesus, please help me.' She had known an abnormal fear of hospitals, doctors, operations, all things medical. For her to contemplate an operation for lung cancer would have been harrowing. On the day she died I knelt and thanked God that she had left this world without knowing the nature of her illness.

'Why didn't the doctors discover it?' a relative asked.

Lung cancer can be hard to detect. With a smoker it might have been suspected, but even if it had been found earlier she would have lived, with an operation, for only a short time.

'The doctors didn't discover it,' I said, 'because God in his goodness hid it from them.' I made this point to my friends. It did not take away the shattering grief but it was a comfort to hang on to in dark days.

We had prayed together regularly. In the following months the prayers which customarily started and ended the day were more intermittent. There was a kind of 'good morning' and 'good night', a reaching upwards, but there was a hurt to be healed, and a measure of self-pity and despair. He did not desert me. Nor do I think he complained at my lack of communication with him. He came, not with a revelation as in St. Paul's Cathedral, but in loving, caring, beautiful friends and neighbours. And because of their love I learned to talk with him again.

If I had not done so I would have resigned from Christian publishing. An editor whose faith has lost its confident and positive note, who spreads gloom and initiates disbelief, is like a running sore. He should not be irremovable.

# 11

# BOOKS CHANGE PEOPLE

'The trouble with these books,' said a Moslem censor, 'is not in any special passage but that everyone who reads them wants to become a Christian.' Christian books are an evangelistic agency second to none. When the missionary has gone on furlough, the sermon ended, the church doors locked, the radio programme concluded, the television picture faded, the books remain.

There is a breathtaking increase in the number of readers throughout the world. Thoughts and actions are influenced by what we read. I constantly meet people whose lives, like my own, have been changed by a book.

I sat in the study of the Reverend Colin Urquhart, who was the parish priest of St. Hugh's, on a large housing estate near Luton. When the bishop had appointed him to the parish he had warned: 'It's a tough job. The first priest had a nervous breakdown and the present vicar's physical health has just given way under strain. There will be a lot of hard work, and it's no use expecting much response. So we would only leave you there for five years: you'll have had enough by then.'

'Some prospect,' Colin Urquhart told himself. After arriving in Luton, before his institution as vicar of the parish, he had two weeks – time to help his wife, Caroline, unpack and get straight. And time to read a book. A book that changed his ministry.

*The Normal Christian Life* was edited from the works of a Chinese Christian, Watchman Nee. In 1952, after foreign missionaries had been expelled from China, Watchman Nee was arrested with other Chinese Christian leaders. He was sentenced to twenty years' imprisonment. The Communists thought they had silenced his ministry. They over-looked his writings.

In addition to the two books he had himself written for publication, *The Spiritual Man* and *The Normal Christian Church Life*, his sermons and lectures had been edited and published. About a dozen were to be translated into English, the best known being *The Normal Christian Life*. As Colin Urquhart read the book he awakened to the fact that nearly everything he had known and experienced about the Christian life was 'sub-normal'.

'I had been taught to be highly suspicious of "experience" and "subjective Christianity". God was often por-trayed to be great, but remote; to be believed in, to be worshipped, but definitely not to be experienced in a personal way. What mattered above everything else was objective truth; that we believed in God's existence and his love.

'Now something happened to me, something that could only be described as "experience" . . . As I read it was like a great flash of light. I had discovered something I had been searching for. I jumped up and shouted, "That's it! That's it! I'm a son of God."'

'But you had been a clergyman for years,' I said.

'Yes, I knew that Jesus Christ died for me but I had not appreciated that when he died I died with him. My old sinful nature had been put to death on the cross. Now I was a new person, free to share a new, risen life with Jesus. I was a son of God, filled with the Holy Spirit. I knew it, not only in my head; my whole being witnessed to it.

'It seemed as if the whole room, the whole house, everyone and everything around me had changed. I wanted to go dancing and skipping round the house shouting, 'I'm a son of God! I'm a son of God. I AM A SON OF GOD.'

'Write a book and tell us what happened and make the first page an account of your reading Watchman Nee,' I urged. 'Tell us about St. Hugh's and of the Know Jesus groups you started.'

'But I've never written a book.'

'We'll edit where necessary.'

*When the Spirit Comes* became an instant bestseller. It had a startling effect on other parishes. He shared how he had found it totally unrealistic to leave all the pastoral work to ordained clergy, how members made a new commitment to each other in love, how the pews filled. Few seemed deterred by the prospect of a Sunday evening service which might last two or three hours.

Meanwhile, Watchman Nee, still a prisoner, died on June 1st, 1972. Ten days before his death he wrote to his sister-in-law in Peking, mentioning his heart complaint, yet declaring, 'the inward joy surpasses everything'.

His books still speak to men.

'No other agency can penetrate so deeply,' wrote Charles Watson, 'abide so persistently, witness so daringly, and influence so irresistibly as the printed page.'

Few Christian authors have been more widely read in the last forty years than C. S. Lewis. He wrote more than fifty books. Most are in print. His Narnia tales are read by children and adults, his science fiction trilogy is reprinted constantly. Some consider *The Screwtape Letters*, *Mere Christianity* and *Surprised by Joy* his most consequential books. Certainly, *The Screwtape Letters* has been the most popular.

In April 1956 he married Joy Davidman Gresham. She and her former husband had been members of the Communist Party in America but turned to Christ after reading the books of Lewis. Soon after her marriage to Lewis, Hodder published her *Smoke on the Mountain*, a notable exposition of the Ten Commandments. C. S. Lewis wrote the foreword. *The Church Times* reviewer pointed out: 'She is by race a Jew, by background an agnostic, by conversion from Communism a member of Christ. She has a mind as glittering and as unyielding as a diamond, and a style as incisive as any sword.'

She had become a Christian in response to her reading, but what turned Lewis himself from atheist to Christian? Among the powerful influences were the writings of George MacDonald and G. K. Chesterton. Of one book by Jakob Boehme he wrote: 'Not like a book at all, but like a thunderclap. Heaven defend us – what things there are knocking about in this world!'

Travelling home on the upper deck of a bus from Magdalen College, he came to the point of crisis: 'I felt myself being, there and then, given a free choice. I could open the door or keep it shut . . . Neither choice was presented as a duty: no threat or promise was attached to either, though I knew that to open the door or take off the corslet meant the incalculable.' Later, in his room at Magdalen, he confessed that God was God. Atheism had turned out to be too simple.

He brought his scholar's mind to face the complexities of Christian doctrine. He turned to an old book, the Bible, reading and re-reading, asking how the life and death of Jesus nearly 2,000 years ago could help us here and now, how there could be a good God and an evil world, why some non-Christians are nicer than Christians.

The outcome was his book *Mere Christianity*, first published in three separate parts *Broadcast Talks* (1942), *Christian Behaviour* (1943), and *Beyond Personality* (1944). His intention he said was not to tell the reader whether to become an Anglican, a Methodist, a Presbyterian, or a Roman Catholic, but to explain the faith to his unbelieving neighbours and to defend the belief that has been common to Christians at all times. He saw the different forms of church services, the various denominations, as rooms leading off the hall. His object was to bring people into the hall. 'If I can bring someone into that hall I shall have done what I attempted. But it is in the rooms, not in the hall, that there are fires and chairs and meals. The hall is a place to wait in, a place from which to try various doors, not a place to live in.'

*Mere Christianity* has helped thousands into the hall of faith. Among them is Charles Colson, former special assistant to President Nixon. The Colson story powerfully demonstrates that books change lives.

I knew little of Chuck Colson until 1975 when John and Elizabeth Sherrill from New York spent an autumn Sunday with Gwen and myself. As co-authors of *The Cross and the Switchblade*, *The Hiding Place* and *God's Smuggler*, we respected them as the finest creative Christian writers.

I had been a guest in their tree-fringed home outside New York, had met them in a house they had rented for a year in Oxford while on a writing assignment, and now I was taking them to three Kentish homes: in the morning to that of my chairman, Philip Attenborough: in the afternoon to Chartwell where Winston Churchill had lived; and then to the bungalow where Tony and Jane Collins were spending their first months of marriage.

As we drove between the homes the topic of conversation altered little. I had been reading Charles Colson's book *Born Again* in manuscript form and I wanted permission to change the title. The Sherrills with Leonard LeSourd and Catherine Marshall had given constructive criticism and encouragement in the writing of the book.

'Titles are important,' I emphasised. '*Born Again* is a Biblical expression but it has become associated with unkempt men who carry poster-boards. It won't help in the high-street bookshops. Because of Watergate this book's going to get television and the national press. That title's a stumbling block.'

I did not know of the debate that had already taken place in America to find the right title. Catherine Marshall and her husband Len LeSourd had spent hours in discussion with Chuck Colson and his wife Patty, considering literally hundreds of suggestions.

When Patty suggested *Born Again* Len LeSourd said, 'It's an overworked Protestant cliché,' but he agreed to try it out on the others. The reaction was cool: it sounded trite, but Colson's conviction deepened and support for it grew.

That day I only knew I failed to persuade a change for the British edition. Gwen listened but did not support me. This was the autumn before her death. Unwell, she sat in the car as we wandered round Chartwell and viewed the rooms where Second World War history was made, where the volumes telling the story of that war had been written. Later, while I was making a telephone call, the Sherrills naturally and spontaneously prayed with her. From their books and those of their close friend, Catherine Marshall, Gwen had long reaped benefit but it was the love and reality of that prayer that held her in the subsequent months.

Before we said goodbye to the Sherrills that evening I confirmed that Hodder would retain the title *Born Again*. Within a year I was thanking God they had not listened to my counsel. Through this book and Colson's spoken testimony the phrase 'born again' was taken from the pulpit into the main street of life. A reporter confronted the presidential candidates: 'Are you born again?' he asked Jimmy Carter. 'Are you born again?' he asked Ronald Reagan.

Two factors had prompted Colson's commitment to Christ: the witness of a prominent businessman and the reading of *Mere Christianity*. His wife had first spotted Colson engrossed in the green and white paperback. He would not put it down, making notes on yellow pads.

'What's in that book you're reading?' she demanded.

'I guess I'm looking for something,' he said. 'I'm trying to find out what's real and what isn't – who we are – who I am in relation to God . . . I'm looking for answers and this little book is terrific.'

He saw that the central thesis of Lewis's book, and the essence of Christianity, is summed up in one sentence: *Jesus Christ is God*. He jotted down, 'Not just part of God, or just sent by God, or just related to God. He was (and therefore, of course, *is*) God.'

He was faced with a choice, stark and frightening: Jesus Christ – lunatic or God? Lewis had put it bluntly like that. If he is not God, he is nothing. Colson wrestled for some days with his lawyer's mind grappling with Lewis's arguments, while the Holy Spirit prepared his heart.

Early one Friday morning, as he sat alone staring at the sea, the words fell naturally from his lips: 'Lord Jesus, I believe you. I accept you. Please come into my life. I commit it to you.'

The critics would accuse him of copping out in time of trouble, of seeking a safe port in the storm, a temporary hiding place. They did. When he came to London for the launching of *Born Again*, before his plane touched down at Heathrow, the cynics were saying, 'He's made his money out of Nixon, now he's going to make a packet out of Jesus,' little knowing the truth.

The cynics were not only in Fleet Street and the Houses of Parliament but in Hodder.

'What's happened,' asked the London *Daily Mail*, 'to the old line about evil-doers getting their deserts and then vanishing into obscurity?' under the headline 'The man who found God in the great American disaster'. *The Church of England Newspaper* commented: 'They do things differently in the U.S.A. Here in the U.K. a man who has misbehaved in a position of high responsibility is expected to keep his head down and rehabilitate himself.' A prominent newspaper reviewer, Peter Owen, declared, 'Those who worship their God with a little more humility can be excused their cynicism at Mr. Colson's redemption and his ability to turn it into a potential bestseller.'

Between my reading his manuscript and the book's publication Gwen died. The weekend Colson came to London I touched bottom.

As he came through customs at London airport with his mother, I recognised him, mid-forties, six feet tall, heavily jowled, with the square look of the successful American businessman. It was how the press had described him. I drove them to their hotel and arranged to meet him on Sunday afternoon to chauffeur him to a speaking engagement.

That Sunday lunchtime I completely broke down in a telephone conversation. There seemed no sense in living. Three hours later I concealed my sorrow from Colson and from Dennis Barker, a columnist on the *Guardian* who asked if he could accompany us on the journey from London to Guildford. He wanted an exclusive interview.

The bulky ex-marine who had shared the back seat of Cadillacs, who sat up with President Nixon to hear the 1972 election results, shrunk himself into my smallish car for what Dennis Barker described as something like 'a barefoot journey to Guildford Baptist Church to tell the flock there how he had discovered Christ'.

In Hammersmith as we began to leave London I took a wrong turning. The *Guardian* told the story.

'Our car was now quite lost somewhere near Richmond. The most efficient fixer of the Western World, circa 1972, clambered out of the car to walk back and consult a road-sign, clutching a map. I also got out clutching another map. With the aid of these ministrations, we shot off in the wrong direction.'

Colson was magnificent. 'Believe me, things like this happened in the White House, as well,' he said. We found the right road and had to make up for lost time. The *Guardian* continued:

'Our car started passing everything on the smeary road, myself half writing notes and half composing myself for my last moments. "I do not feel a bit afraid," said Colson. "I never have, since my experience of Christ."'

We arrived in time to join the Baptist deacons in prayer before the service began.

Next day, Hodder's Eric Major, travelled by train with Colson to Scotland for live television. Eric had shared with me his hesitations about Nixon's former hatchet man. He had read *Time* magazine's description: 'Tough, wily, nasty and tenaciously loyal to Nixon.'

Two days later Eric returned from Scotland all doubts assuaged. He had talked with Colson for hours on the journey – he was quite convinced of his sincerity.

'The man who once spat orders at his staff,' a journalist wrote after an interview, 'and brooked nothing less than total obedience to Nixon's cause, is today mild-mannered and quiet-spoken.'

'Here is,' said Dr. William Barclay, 'one of the greatest conversion stories of the modern world.'

Witness the pattern of books changing people; C. S. Lewis influenced by George Macdonald and G. K. Chesterton; Charles Colson coming to commitment after reading C. S. Lewis's *Mere Christianity*. And now, today, people being changed by reading *Born Again*. Colson received hundreds of letters. One from a couple who had been reconciled after both of them were given copies by friends; from prisoners who found new life in Christ while serving their sentence; from a senator who broke his ties with an underground Communist organisation and started again.

'*Born Again*', one reader wrote, 'has stirred me with hope that I can find meaning and purpose for my life. I have never been moved to such emotion on the subject of faith and Christ.' Colson replied immediately. A few weeks later he received a second letter: 'The past five weeks have been the most remarkable and wonderful weeks of my life.'

I was honoured to be associated with such writing. Now whenever I find myself meeting a Colin Urquhart or a Charles Colson I find myself echoing the words of Job: 'How forcible are right words . . . Oh, that they were printed in a book!'

# 12

# FINDING A TITLE

The final choice of a book title may be the publisher's. The author will have a working title as he writes the manuscript. It may change a dozen times in his mind as he writes his 50,000 or 70,000 words. By the day he delivers the complete manuscript he will have reached a pitch of uncertainty. An authoritative, instant recommendation from the publisher may clinch the matter.

But publishers can be wrong. I have demonstrated that with Charles Colson's *Born Again*, where I inadvisedly recommended another title. With another distinguished author I was wrong on two occasions. Let me tell the story.

In 1969 I wrote to Cardinal John Heenan, Archbishop of Westminster, with the suggestion that I commissioned a biography of him. He replied with an invitation to tea, so I did some hasty research into his life.

For many years his desire to become a priest had been a secret betwen his mother and himself. He was ordained in 1930 and during the war was parish priest in Manor Park, in London's East End. He remained there throughout the war in which not one house in his parish was undamaged. In 1947, he was appointed Superior of the Catholic Missionary Society. He was consecrated Bishop of Leeds in 1951, Archbishop of Liverpool in 1957, and Archbishop of Westminster in 1963.

The prospect of tea with a Cardinal Archbishop made me nervous. On my way to his apartments I called to see Graham Jenkins, manager of Westminster Cathedral bookshop, and a friend of the Cardinal's for a quick briefing. Graham was my favourite Catholic bookseller as Alan Maynard, of the E.C.L. Bookshop in Bristol, was my number one evangelical bookseller. A book mysteriously had an extra quality if it were bought from either of them. Graham advised me to relax. 'He's kind, he's courteous, he's understanding,' he said. 'And extra so to non-Catholics.'

Over tea I talked with the Cardinal of his ordination. 'I remember every detail,' he said. 'The ordination ceremony was and has remained the great spiritual experience of my life.' He passed the dainty sandwiches, then reached for a photograph of his mother. 'As a boy when I was late, ill-tempered, greedy, untidy or otherwise unbearable she would remind that if I was to become a priest I had to be punctual, good-tempered, unselfish, tidy and, in general, insufferably virtuous.'

'Is she still alive?' I asked.

'She died on June 8th, 1949,' he said, as if it were yesterday. 'I'll tell you about it. In May 1949 I began my first prison mission. It was in Walton Gaol, Liverpool. The opening sermon in any mission is important but for a prison mission it needs to be a masterpiece. Within hours the whole prison knows whether the missioner is worth hearing. The first thing is to remove suspicion.'

He told them the mission wasn't aimed at just them. It was a mission to the whole country – why should they be left out? The mission would be the same as any other he conducted, with one difference – there would be no collection! After that first service he was called to the telephone to speak to his brother. This was unusual, as the family made it a rule never to 'phone when he was taking a mission. The news was bad.

His mother had been taken ill and was not expected to recover. She had told his brother not to telephone because, she said, the men in prison needed him more than she did. His brother had disregarded her wishes because he felt that he would want to be with her. In this, of course, he was right, but the Cardinal told me he felt his mother was also right in saying that the men needed him more. He decided to stay in Walton.

Next morning he told the prisoners about the phone call and asked them to join with him in praying that he would be able to finish the mission and still be in time to see his mother before she died. During the day his mother was the topic of discussion in the prison. The prison chaplain shared with him that the men were scandalised that he had not hurried home. They thought he must be unnatural.

Before preaching his sermon that night he put the facts plainly to the men. His mother, he told them, had no fear of death and did not need him. She had expressly forbidden any member of the family to let him know that she was so ill. She had been praying for this Walton mission for weeks – in fact she would be praying for the men at this very moment. She was convinced that the mission must go on. Who was he to contradict her? As a son he wanted to be with his dying mother but, also as a son, he did not want to refuse her dying wish. He asked for their prayers every night during the week that he would be with his mother at the end.

'What was their response?' I asked.

As he went from cell to cell, he recalled, the prisoners assured him of their prayers. His mother's prayers were heard. This was, so far as he could judge, the most fruitful mission he ever had. The men's prayers were also heard. His mother remained alive for a week after the mission and he was alone with her when she died.

'Were any men converted?' I asked, wondering if that was a Salvation Army rather than a Catholic question.

'Many were,' he said. 'I'll show you a letter I received nineteen years after the mission.'

It was dated January 24th, 1968, and read:

I was in Walton prison, Liverpool, many years ago and you conducted a mission there. I was deeply moved at the time when you told us how your mother before her death told you not to cancel the mission and return home because we needed you more than she did. You can be sure that we prayed hard for you at that time. My point in writing is that I wish you to know that this mission bore fruit and I have settled down with a good job for many years now. I feel that the mission was the turning point in my life.

I brought him back to the purpose of my visit. A biography? I named two or three professional authors whom I had mentioned earlier to Graham Jenkins.

'How much of my time will they need?' he asked, open to the proposal of a book. Thousands of Catholics and many public library readers would welcome it. After talking for a further half hour, to my delight, he decided it would be less trouble to write an autobiography than to answer a thousand and one questions from a biographer. It was more than I had dreamed. He was an accomplished writer: in his first years as a priest he had contributed to the national press and to numerous periodicals. He had written a well-reviewed biography, *Cardinal Hinsley*.

The writing occupied him during holidays and convalescence over the next two years. When the manuscript was finished I received a second invitation to tea.

'There'll have to be two volumes,' he apologised handing me more than 400 large typewritten sheets. 'This book only takes me to my appointment as Bishop of Leeds. Does it matter?'

'No publisher minds having two bestsellers instead of one,' I said. 'What do you propose calling Volume One?'

'*Not the Whole Truth*', he replied 'Do you like it?'

I shook my head. It might be an apt description of any autobiography but why highlight it on the jacket?

'Have you an alternative, Cardinal Heenan?'

'Let me explain why I've called it that,' he said. Then he added graciously, 'If you still don't like it I'll think again.' I declined another cup of tea and he settled back in his chair.

'After thirty years cabinet ministers are at liberty to reveal any secrets their colleagues may not have already disclosed in their memoirs. Some do it after five or so years. Ministers of Christ must keep confidences without limit of time. Whether or not they are of his flock, many people turn in confidence to the priest to discuss their intimate problems. This is one reason why I cannot give the whole truth. The priest is only a steward and it is required of a steward that he must be trustworthy.'

'I'll put that on the book jacket,' I responded warmly. 'It's a great title.'

'Nobody, I think, will feel betrayed by what I have

recorded,' he said. 'Of course it would have been possible to tell much more of the truth about myself but that would have required great humility.'

While writing the second volume the Cardinal was extremely ill. Two years passed and I wondered if he would live to complete the work, then the invitation came again to call on him. The manuscript was ready. I found him frail but as considerate as ever.

'I wonder if you'll like the title this time,' he said, with a smile, remembering our last discussion.

I waited and said nothing.

'*A Crown of Thorns*', he said, watching my face.

'It sounds a bit too Catholic.'

'I'll explain. Then you decide. On a day just before the war I was summoned to Westminster. When I arrived I found Cardinal Hinsley in his room trying on a new mitre. In playful mood he put it on my head. It fitted perfectly. The Cardinal's face became serious. "One day," he said, "you'll wear a mitre of your own and you'll find it a crown of thorns." I have. My happiest days were as a parish priest.' He paused. 'Will you accept my title?'

'It's great,' I said. 'We'll call it *A Crown of Thorns*'.

The second volume was longer than the first. Throughout the record of his years as Bishop of Leeds, Archbishop of Liverpool and Archbishop of Westminster was the realisation that the sacrifice a bishop has to make is to give up most of the direct and intimate contact with ordinary parishioners. 'You will become acquainted with heads of organisations,' he wrote, 'mayors, Members of Parliament, doctors, matrons and directors of education. But you will no longer know the Christian names of the school children.'

Nevertheless, he enjoyed high office and the privileges associated with it. He was a well equipped and able managing director of the Catholic Church. His successor, Cardinal Basil Hume, a monk and former Abbot of Ampleforth, would not claim the same management skills but he has something greater. He has captured the public imagination with what a journalist described as 'his holiness, engaging humility, penetrating intelligence, welcoming friendliness'.

106

On the day of his appointment I wrote and asked Basil Hume if I might meet him when he took up residence in London. I waited a few months for an appointment. He was not going to write an autobiography. Nor, at that point, was he willing to give support for a biography, but if I cared to join him for coffee one morning . . . Over that beverage, a little reluctantly, he was persuaded to share with me the scripts of the talks he had given to the monastic community at Ampleforth.

I read them on a train journey to Salisbury. 'Holy, holy, holy' seemed engraved on the pages. Here was a man who acknowledged the Lordship of Christ, who worshipped at his feet, who told the novitiates:

> Your function is threefold. First, you have to get to know God and him whom he has sent: Jesus Christ our Lord . . . Secondly, you have to get to know yourself, and there will be little chance of escaping. You have to face up to what you are; and the discovery may be disconcerting, even alarming. Thirdly, you have to get to know one another . . . This knowledge of God, yourself, and your neighbour should lead you to a threefold loving: a love of God, of yourself, and of the brethren.

I said amen. There were differences in our theology, and theology matters, but a living Christ united us.

A selection of these talks taken from an accumulation of conferences extending over a period of thirteen years was compiled by Father Felix Stephens, O.S.B., Elizabeth Hamilton, an accomplished biographer, was chosen to edit the language, where necessary, into a more formal style, suited to the written word.

There was no question over the title of this book. I do not recall how it originated, but all who saw the manuscript immediately accepted *Searching for God*. It was to become, for eighteen months, the number-one religious bestseller.

Today I find myself returning to the section of the book 'Life in the Spirit', meditating on it as an inspiration to prayer. Within the best religious communities there is an awareness and an experience of intercession which those of us in the busy world long to share.

The Cardinal described prayer as:

An act of faith: 'Lord, we would have our eyes opened.' As an act of love. 'You know all things, Lord, you you know that I love you.'

Prayer is the cry of a humble man: one who recognises his inadequacy before God. 'Lord, be merciful to me a sinner.'

Prayer is the cry also of someone who is grateful . . . A humble man is a grateful man . . . Prayer is the song of one who strives to see the majesty and beauty of God; who can admire the wonders of the created universe in order to wonder at the Creator whose majesty and beauty those created things mirror. It is a song of response from one who has reflected on the greatness of God's love for him and who strives to return love for love.

Some evangelical friends were surprised to receive from me a Christmas copy of this book. James Packer they knew, Michael Green and Martyn Lloyd-Jones they knew, but a Catholic Cardinal? Months later one of them shared that *Searching for God* had become his prime bedside book. 'Hardly a day passes without my turning to it,' he confided. 'Often I need read only a paragraph.' My old bookshop, the Scripture Union, displayed it prominently with other new publications, and quickly sold more than fifty copies. Barriers which had existed for centuries were disappearing as believers found common meeting ground. In the words of Thomas Smail in an editorial in *Renewal*: 'The rich unity that God has for us consists in the fellowship of Roman Christians, Anglican Christians, Baptist Christians, Pentecostal Christians and the rest who have not left their treasures behind them, but who have purified and made their own what God gave to their fathers and now come to give and to receive across all the breached barriers of the past.'

'The time is coming,' I told Tony Collins, 'when it may be possible for my ambition to be fulfilled. To put three Christian authors, each from a different tradition, on a small boat for a round-the-world voyage. We'll publish the log on their return.'

'Which three?'

'The ones I'd prefer may be too old for the adventure,' I said, 'but what about the General of the Salvation Army, Cardinal Basil Hume and Dr. Billy Graham?'

'It would make a marvellous film,' he said.

# 13

# IN THE COLD

Without Gwen I turned to books to discover about running
a home. A secretary with a sense of humour gave me *A
Brownie's First Cook Book*. From other sources I found, in
an amateurish fashion, how to shop, vacuum, wash clothes
and iron. I did not learn how to hang out the washing on the
clothes-line. None of my books explained that. On my first
wash-day I tried, with some satisfaction, but the comments
of a neighbour made me give up. After that I dried the
clothes indoors.

Holidays. What does one do? Sit on a beach alone? Go
on a coach tour and share a seat for long days with a
talkative traveller?

'Take advantage of being single,' a friend suggested
intelligently. 'Do something you wouldn't do if you were
married.'

The idea stuck. I liked it. It projected my thoughts into
the future. What should I do? Where should I go? Why no
encounter the unknown?

I walked up London's Regent Street looking at
brochures in airline and shipping offices, one minute con
templating East Africa, the next South America. Near
Broadcasting House was the Russian Intourist Trave
Agency. I made a booking for Siberia.

For ten years I had made a practice of visiting authors in
their own homes. One or two were grand places, in park
like settings, with gardeners and domestic staff. Most were
full of character and books but comparatively modest. In
Siberia there was an author I had not met but had long
admired – Georgi Vins. He was in a labour camp in one of
the coldest spots on earth. His book, *Three Generations of*

*Suffering*, had been 'smuggled' out. He was the third generation of his family to be imprisoned for being a Christian believer who did not conform to the State's requirements.

It was unlikely I would be able to visit him in his camp or to do anything to benefit him, but by travelling in his country I would gain a limited understanding of his situation; experience the climate, see the landscape, meet a few citizens. Vins was in the Yakutia region, which had been called Siberia *in extremis*. Half of it lies inside the Arctic Circle and nearly all of it is permanently frozen, in summer and winter. There are more reindeer than men, which is hardly surprising in a place where the sun can disappear for ten weeks at a stretch, and where rivers freeze for ten months.

At five o'clock on a chill January morning I dragged myself from bed to complete my packing: long woollen pants, five layers of clothing, fur hat, two pairs of gloves, 35mm camera, and the *Fodor Guide*. I had mentally underlined its advice.

Don't photograph any military object, any port, hydro-electrical establishment, radio station, telephone offices, scientific institutions, or even bridges . . . Don't take photographs from airplanes or trains . . . If you intend taking closeups of people, ask them . . . After that, if you haven't lost the nerve, shoot away!

There had been a 'phone call from Pastor Richard Wurmbrand's son, Mihai, the previous evening. He was speaking from Los Angeles.

'Watch out for girls they may put in your way,' he said.

'I might come back with a Russian wife.'

'Be careful.'

I laughed unbelievingly.

'I don't understand,' he said, 'when half the people in Russian want to get out, you're going there.'

At the last minute I picked up Dostoevsky's *The Possessed*, Malcolm Muggeridge's recommendation for the Trans-Siberian train, and Laurens van der Post's *Journey into Russia*. I was off.

111

The customs officer at Moscow airport did not exude goodwill. He examined the contents of my suitcase, perhaps because it had 'editor' on my passport, not for drugs but for books. He started with the notebook, which I intended to use as a diary, and finished by riveting his gaze on the Penguin *Journey into Russia*.

'Is this yours?' he asked.

'Yes,' I replied. I had borrowed it from Rob Fowles, Hodder's chief accountant. It was not offensive. The author had written about the airport. 'I detected no sign of rigidity, arrogance or suspiciousness in my own reception. It is true there were still no smiles and the customs and immigration officials, leaning casually against their counters, looked almost indifferent. They stamped my declaration forms without reading them and passed my bag without opening it.' I was not so fortunate.

'Why've you brought it?' he demanded.

'As a guide. To read as I travel.'

The other passengers had left the customs hall and joined the coach destined for Central Moscow. He opened more pages, distrust in his eyes, while my unease deepened. I had casually examined the book before packing it. It was well-informed, unprejudiced, balanced by Western standards.

'You'll wait here,' he ordered.

I might, after all, be meeting Georgi Vins! The *Fodor Guide* had listed goods it was prohibited to import, ranging from weapons and ammunition to printed matter 'harmful to the U.S.S.R. politically or economically'. Russian authors who had not written to the State's directives had been pilloried, imprisoned, put in mad-houses, as had Christians who sought more liberty.

There was a story concerning those who smuggled Bibles into Russia.

'Why do you get so upset about Bibles being brought into your country?' a Russian colonel was asked.

'Because it's a book of fairy stories.'

'Don't you have fairy stories in Russia?'

'Yes, we do.'

'Then what's wrong with another?'

'If they believe in the Bible,' the colonel replied, 'then

112

they'll not believe in Communism any more.'

The customs man returned with a senior officer. The atmosphere was heavy with fear and suspicion. They systematically went through the book's index and the chapter headings. The Communist *Daily Worker*'s reviewer had found it, 'Honest, full of delightful vignettes of Soviet life brought out with a subtle sense of humour.'

The senior officer closed the book, threw it in my case and closed the lid. 'You may go,' he said. I hurriedly caught the coach, now questioning the wisdom of my intended day-by-day diary. Would they read that before I left?

I stayed the night at the National Hotel, overlooking the Kremlin, off Gorki Street. Next morning I joined a tour of Central Moscow, catching a glimpse of the Lenin State Library, with its twenty-seven million books and 10,000 borrowers a day. Unescorted, I visited a large bookshop but could not browse, every book being behind the counters. I stared at the notorious Lubyanka prison which, in Stalin's day, even casual shoppers hurried past, knowing it was often a first stop to Siberia.

The night flight to Khabarovsk in the Soviet Far East left at eight forty-five that evening. By dawn we were over Siberia, an expanse of forests and frozen rivers with an absence of roads. Rivers had been the means of access into parts of the interior before aeroplanes and helicopters.

My thoughts were of Georgi Vins. Pressure was being put upon the Russian embassies in Europe and Washington for his release. I remembered his sickness, due to an inadequate diet and harsh conditions, as the air hostess brought breakfast.

In Khabarovsk the sky was so blue and the sun so bright that the intense cold came as a shock. I spent three days in the city before boarding the Trans-Siberian train but only one incident was of significance.

Three other Englishmen were in my hotel, and the four of us hired a car to get a glimpse of the *taiga*, the forest which stretches for thousands of miles. Once out of the city there was no green, only white, everywhere. From the warm car interior it was beautiful.

We reached a nature reserve with a locked gate but in the timber cottage, logs piled high by the door, the driver found a peasant woman with a key. She was obviously displeased at being disturbed but gathered her shawls around her, stumbled through the snow and unlocked it for us. Thirty minutes later, when we returned, she had taken her revenge. The gate was locked; the cottage empty.

We were stuck, miles from anywhere, with no alternative exit. If we turned off the engine, within minutes we would freeze. Could we get the car down the embankment and round the gate?

'It'll overturn,' I said, thinking I would not risk my own car, but there was no choice. The driver remained in his seat, while the four of us stood by to steady the car as it slid down the slope in bottom gear. It tipped over the edge. With superhuman strength we stopped it toppling over. Ten minutes later we were off.

The car rocked over the twisting ice-packed roads. There was no space for a vehicle to pass: there were none. We paused at a road junction with four exits and no sign post, took the wrong turn and had to reverse half a mile. The driver did not appear to regard the roads as hazardous. Hot air blowing on the screen prevented it from freezing but the side and rear windows were completely iced up.

Abruptly, we all stopped talking.

There are prison camps throughout Siberia: there was one ahead; we had accidently stumbled on it. The barbed wire fencing, the long, low wooden huts, the guards, the wolf-like dogs outside the gates, matched the photographs. It was the rear exit of a camp.

The driver looked straight ahead. We did not speak. Two dogs bounded towards us, jumping at the side of the car, their sharp barks echoing in the forest. When we had the courage, we asked:

'What was that?'

The driver said nothing.

'With the barbed wire and the dogs?'

'I didn't see,' he mumbled.

'Not the guards?'

None of us pressed him further, but the picture stayed with me. I visualised Georgi Vins living in such a place. When I fell asleep my dreams were frightening, but the telephone interrupted. I stumbled out of bed. It rang every

114

night I was in a Russian hotel. I picked it up. Having established my presence the caller rang off.

It is the longest railway line in the world. It stretches for 5,778 miles, from the Pacific coast of Siberia to Moscow. It was built between 1890 and 1900. Foreigners are not allowed to board it at Vladivostok, a military port, where it starts, so Khabarovsk had to be my boarding point.

The train had travelled 564 miles when it pulled into the station shortly after one p.m. as the timetable predicted. The Trans-Siberian, whatever the climatic conditions, however heavy the snow, was punctual.

The carriage attendant, a slim ashen-faced woman, had my name and showed me to a compartment, giving me sheets and pillowcase. The sexes were not segregated in the four-berth compartments. I had been put with three men – the English travellers – but a surprise was in store.

Between Khabarovsk and Moscow there were seventy-nine stops, many of two minutes duration. The first was at Birabiszhan, a Jewish settlement. The population was 40,000. It was near the Chinese border, frozen in winter, plagued by mosquitoes in summer. The Jews who had been exiled there had dug up large areas of the *taiga*, cleared construction sites and turned up untrodden land. They produced power transformers, tin, cement, lime, paper, furniture, knitted goods, clothing and footwear.

Siberia did not flow with milk and honey, but they had made this Jewish Autonomous Region so productive, they had been awarded the Order of Lenin.

I was sitting on a fold-down seat in the corridor, having swopped chocolate with a child for a brooch celebrating sixty years of Soviet rule in the Far East, when a dark-haired young woman appeared.

She might have been simply going to pass by but her approach suggested I was her objective.

I was only halfway through the first chapter of Dostoevsky's *The Possessed*. I kept my eyes on the page, not reading. She had stopped and was looking through the window into the night. The lights of Birabiszhan had disappeared. There was only her own reflection. I turned a page, alert to her. Twenty-seven? A Soviet citizen who

115

spoke English? She was looking at me but I kept my head down.

A few yards away the car attendant brewed tea in her cramped quarters, having stoked the fire at the end of the corridor. The fire, the linen, refilling the tea-glasses, dealing with drunks, reporting on passengers kept her busy. She was three or four years older than the pretty girl but in appearance they were worlds apart. For her the train was home.

The pretty girl was touching her hair. Why shouldn't I smile? She needed no other bidding and came towards me. 'Excuse me,' she said, 'you're English?'

I stood up, put out my hand, and nodded.

'You speak English well,' I said.

'I'd like to,' she replied softly. 'If I could travel with you to Moscow it would improve.'

An alarm bell rang in my head.

'I'm getting off at Irkutsk on Thursday,' I apologised standing back to let a huddled peasant woman in black reach the toilets. They were a disgrace; no paper, no towel, no soap, no hot water.

'My name's Valentina.'

'Mine's Edward.'

'I teach English at the Railway Institute in Khabarovsk,' she said.

'I'm a publisher. Is your family in Moscow?'

'I've no one there. I'm going for further studies. To improve my English,' she beamed. 'What's your book?'

I handed it over and she approved.

'Is this your compartment? Is there a spare bunk?'

'No, it's full.'

'I'm along the train but there may be an empty bunk elsewhere in this carriage. I could move.'

'Are you allowed?'

'Yes,' her eyes sparkled.

Was she a teacher, did she work at the Railway Institute, or had she been planted? She was poised, intelligent; if she taught English it was natural for her to seek out a passenger from England.

Through the compartment window the other Englishmen were watching. Paul, the youngest, in his late twenties,

116

pushed back the door and said hullo. The others followed. They shook hands formally and we hustled her inside.

'Watch out for agent provocateurs,' the *Fodor Guide* warned. But this seemed a decent girl, one who might live next door. She glowed at the conquest of four Englishmen. She stayed with us, sitting on the bunk, until eleven that night and returned before breakfast in the morning.

She had moved to the next compartment and became part of the rhythm of our journey. If she were a KGB plant that sinister organisation had chosen well. She was tailor-made for Englishmen, a happy distraction through the endless *taiga*. Was her role surveillance, to indoctrinate, to compromise? We welcomed her presence and forgot about the intention.

'Are you married?' we asked her.

'Yes.'

'A family?'

'A girl. She's four. I've left her and my husband in Khabarovsk.'

'You'll miss them.'

'I'm happy to be going to Moscow.' It was not a lie. She relished the Trans-Siberian train.

By the second day she had found out the essentials about each of us; the sales director from Edinburgh; Jim, from Lancashire who had been in the army in the First World War; Paul, unmarried, a railway enthusiast, from Surrey. She had quizzed me about Gwen's death and the long months since.

'Why doesn't Russia give Jews and Christians freedom to worship as they wish?' I asked.

'We do.' She was offended. 'There's freedom. Except for those sects which harm their children.'

'There are Baptists in prison.' I did not mention Vins by name, for others were in prison, and had been forbidden Bibles or Gospels on the grounds that they were pernicious books.

'Today,' she said, ignoring my comment, 'we are too scientifically educated to believe in God. In our villages there are a few believers, but not in the cities. God is an out of date concept.'

'No,' I replied. 'And not even in Russia. Atheism is the

117

philosophy of the State, but thousands still pray to God daily. They know from their experience that God is.'

'You go to church?' she asked.

'On Sunday.'

'But you're not old, or sick.' She paused and looked thoughtful. 'But go to church if it gives you comfort. Until you find another wife.' She waited for my response. I said nothing. 'Marry a girl in her twenties.'

I laughed, knowing she was changing the topic. 'That's too young.'

'How old are you? Forty?'

'Forty-five,' I said appreciatively.

'Is there a girl you'd like to marry?'

'She'd have to be a Christian.'

She looked through the window into the darkness and saw her own profile reflected. Had there been any Christians in her family, I wondered, years ago? Did she ever pray? For her family before she went to sleep? Had she met a real Christian like the Russian Baptist who wrote:

> My God
> is everywhere, alive in
> town, village, fields, the endless woods,
> capturing our hearts
> and setting them free from sin.

For more than 1,000 miles the land had been flat, with a few scattered hamlets of primitive wooden houses, logs high in the garden, essential for survival. A single track road ran alongside the railway but miles went by without a lorry or car. At the tiny stations, the agile, braver passengers nipped out for bread, cigarettes, milk, providing their own refreshments, not using the restaurant car. Without porters or flags or whistles, the train hooted and went. At Chita, where the timetable announced a fifteen-minute stop, Valentina jumped out with us for a photograph, but the driver brushed us away when he saw the camera near his engine. Here there was a switch from a diesel to an electric locomotive.

With my camera Jim took a photograph of me sitting inside the carriage. It was forbidden. A Soviet passenger

118

saw as she passed along the corridor and made a report. A stocky man, fur hat on, appeared and demanded an explanation.

'It's only an interior shot,' I explained.

He focused his gaze.

'No more photographs. Or your camera will be confiscated.'

Valentina explained that our photograph, although inside the carriage, might have included a shot of a passing train. At intervals these passed by, long goods wagons covered with tarpaulin.

At Yablonovka the scenery changed from birch trees to mountainous terrain and frozen rivers. There was little wild life, hardly a bird, and even fewer people, although a fur-clad hunter tracking with his gun brought us to the window. Over-hunting had reduced the animal population, skins fetching a high price in the sales. Fur-bearing animals were almost as valuable as gold. I saw only sheep, some bony cows, and dogs. Livestock demanded heated shelter for six months of the year.

The train averaged less than forty miles an hour and did not justify the name Express. The winters were so severe that the track could not be maintained for higher speeds. At every stop the ice was broken off the train's brakes, usually by red-faced, big-muscled women, bulging in warm clothing.

Valentina and Paul had struck up a friendship and taken to standing in the corridor. In the dining-car he allowed no one else to settle her bill. A Russian businessman unsuccessfully competed for her attention.

I thought of Ann. I had met her only a few times. The first occasion was clear in my mind, nearly seven years before. She was then studying for membership of the Royal College of Obstetricians and Gynaecologists, before returning to a missionary hospital in Thailand. She secured her membership and spent a further term in Manorom. Now she had left the Overseas Missionary Fellowship and was working in a London Hospital.

We had met once for dinner since Gwen died and I had asked if I might telephone her on my return. She had grown up in Cornwall, becoming a committed Christian while at medical school in Cardiff. She was beautiful and gentle, and six years younger than myself.

The train's movement had become part of our life. It was cosy and comfortable, if restricted; the dark outside – and it seemed mostly dark – wrapped itself around us. I stood in the corridor at Chita, a major junction, near the Gobi region, on the doorstep of Mongolia. It used to be the connecting line for the Chinese railway and Peking. We were nearer to Peking than to Khabarovsk.

It was my last night on the train. We had talked with Valentina about literature, China, the defence of Lenigrad, abortion and the Kremlin. There had been no banned topic. At seven sixteen a.m. on Thursday I said goodbye. She stood at the open door and waved. The temperature in Irkutsk was thirty-five below freezing.

A porter with a sledge took my luggage, pulling it across the shadowy platform. Georgi Vins was probably breaking the ice to wash himself at the start of this day.

The Hotel in Irkutsk was modern, built for Intourist, with five lifts and a stone staircase for people in a hurry. After three nights on the train I was like a swaying sailor stepping ashore. The sensation wore off after a shower, a shave and an hour's sleep, and the single room was heavenly after the train. I was scheduled for breakfast at nine thirty: pancakes and sour cream.

Irkutsk is the capital of a territory larger than France, Holland, Belgium, Switzerland and Denmark put together, but with a population of only two and a half million. It is five hours' flight from Moscow.

This was the nearest point on my itinerary to Yakutia where Pastor Vins was serving his sentence. Could I make the journey there? The Intourist office was polite but definite. Yakutia was out of bounds. I must not travel more than thirty miles outside the cities listed on my documents.

Vins' father had served three terms of imprisonment in a Stalinist labour camp. *Three Generations of Suffering* contained the prison diary Vins had kept between 1966 and 1969, and an account of his mother's imprisonment between 1970 and 1973. Georgi Vins had written:

My Darling Mother!

Thirty-three years ago you saw your husband – my father – off on his last prisoner's journey, and now my children have seen you off. It is hard for me to realise that you are in prison. You are old and sick, living under such a burden of suffering . . . What crime have you ever committed? In your old age you stood up in defence of those persecuted for their faith . . . Your persecutors could not forgive you for this . . . I preserved your letters and read them through time and time again, sitting on my plank-bed. My heart flooded with renewed spiritual power and hope in the Lord!

There was one church open in Irkutsk. I made my way there with a guide and asked to buy a Bible. There are no Bibles on sale in the 14,000 State bookshops but the Russian Orthodox Church had been allowed to print a limited edition in Moscow in 1966.

There were only pictures and ikons on the stall in the church but from a rear room a Bible was produced, well-bound in hard covers.

'How much, please?'

'Fifty roubles.'

I laughed.

'That's about £70,' I objected. 'What's a New Testament cost?'

'Thirty-five roubles.'

'If the State produced them they would cost five roubles,' the guide explained. 'See how the church profiteers!'

That night, troubled about some statements in my diary, I awoke before it was light and quietly made my way to the bathroom and removed five pages. I tore them into tiny shreds and flushed them away.

On Saturday I saw the church of St. Nicholas, by Lake Baikal, an hour's drive through the *taiga*. The weekly service was at five p.m. There were eight elderly peasants present, in grey and black shawls, lighting the candles, kissing ikons, bowing to the ground. The reflection of the sun through a high window added to the beauty of their devotions.

The sun was setting as I walked the mile along the frozen

121

river back to the road where transport was waiting. Ahead was the vast expanse of Lake Baikal, with ships and boats frozen in, like the photographs I had seen of Antarctica.

I flew to Bratsk for two days. There, at three o'clock in the morning, unable to sleep, I prepared the talk I was to give the next week at the banquet for the Christian Booksellers' Convention in London. The other speaker was Marabel Morgan, author of *The Total Woman*. How could I follow her? I would talk about Siberia and Georgi Vins, of a faith that survived Soviet prison camps and temperatures that fell sixty below freezing. I had been unable to do anything for him. No one could, but I could urge prayer for his release and for others like him. Although my bedroom was warm I could not see through the frozen window. Out there, unseen, God was with him, and God saw.*

I returned to Moscow to find that the temperature was only nine below freezing. It seemed like spring. At the Bolshoi I had booked to see *Ivan the Terrible*. It was there I had my alarming moment.

I handed my overcoat to a cloakroom attendant and crossed the crowded foyer between groups of immaculately-groomed men with their beautifully-gowned ladies, towards a magnificent staircase. The elegance was disturbing after the poverty of Siberia, but I wanted to revel in this evening.

A hand rested on my shoulder. In London I would have turned expecting to greet a friend, in New York to be invited to dinner. In Moscow, my unspoken, unconfessed, neurotic fears solidified. This was it. The publisher of Richard Wurmbrand and Georgi Vins was being detained.

I turned. A darkly-dressed man spoke in Russian. A representative of the KGB? I spoke in English. He did not understand. He took my arm. No one noticed as he discreetly led me back across the foyer. He paused at the cloakroom. The curtain would rise in fifteen minutes. Where would I be?

He looked at my ticket and pointed to the gallery. I had inadvertently used the VIP cloakroom.

* He was released and allowed to leave Russia in April 1979.

122

# 14

# THE MYTH

'Can Hodder pull out the stops and publish a book in three weeks?' The telephone caller was Canon Michael Green, of St. Aldate's, Oxford.

'Michael,' I protested, 'at this moment there are 150 other new books going through our production department. The normal publishing process takes nine months. Did you say three weeks?'

It is a lengthy procedure, not fully appreciated by authors, which takes a manuscript and turns it into an attractive book on display in the high streets of the world. First, the typewritten pages go through the copy-editing department. Experienced authors can be inconsistent – for example, in the use of capitals, or quotation marks, or in the style of footnotes. The copy-editor, with an eye for detail, spots inaccuracies which a hard-pressed senior editor has missed. Copy-editing a book can take from three days to three weeks.

The copy-edited manuscript goes to the production manager, when decisions are finalised with the editor about the format of the book, the quality of paper and binding, the jacket design – in full colour with illustration, or plain, good lettering in two or three colours. An estimated print number is agreed, to be finalised nearer publication. The production manager, with a background in printing, will have views on the design of the page and the typeface to be used. He will seek competitive estimates from three or four printers. These can vary by thousands of pounds. A printer who is short of work will cut his price, a printer over-loaded may be prohibitive.

Will there be an index? Who will prepare it? How many pages should be left for its insertion at proof stage? Most authors prepare their own index but professional indexers are available.

While the printer does the type-setting, the sales department and the publicity manager will discuss a marketing plan with the editorial chiefs. Are showcards, brochures, additional proofs for booksellers, extra jackets required? How many review copies? If it is a religious book it must go to the *Church Times* but what about *The Daily Telegraph*? Between 125 and 300 copies of each new title are given away for review and publicity purposes. A dozen or more may be requested for radio and television producers.

Soon the author will be receiving his proofs. He will ask for between three weeks and a month to read them and, hopefully, he will resist the temptation to rewrite. His contract has a penalty clause if he does.

The subsidiary rights manager, or the author's literary agent, meanwhile will be negotiating serialisation in a newspaper or magazine, American rights, possible translations, and showing a manuscript or set of proofs to book clubs. There may be plans for an edition in braille for which no charge is made by publisher or author. With a book like *The Hiding Place*, by Corrie ten Boom, there will be film negotiations.

The salesmen, with catalogues and proofs of the book jackets will be visiting booksellers, wholesalers and librarians in Britain, Australia, New Zealand, South Africa, Canada and other overseas markets. If authors are the life-blood of publishing the booksellers are the arteries. Where would we be without them – secular and Christian? A few Christian bookshops remain 'precious' in a fashion which causes cultured readers to turn away, but more and more are being run by men and women of professional competence, who operate licensed book agencies in churches, youth clubs, and schools; who annually bring themselves up-to-date at trade conferences and by attending the Christian Booksellers' Convention. Most live modestly, some sacrificially, putting their profits into stock on their shelves, rather than into comfortable life-styles. They are an integral part of church-life, affecting the character of their community. Our survival as publishers depends on them.

As publication day draws near the publicity department will seek author interviews on television and radio and in the newspapers, and consider a press conference. They will plan the press advertising.

With such a programme nine months becomes a reasonable period. There are publishers who take longer. Michael Green was asking if we could publish a book in three weeks.

'Why the awful panic?' I asked. There were religious authors who had put Hodder under similar pressure when they believed the Second Coming was imminent.

'We want to write and publish an instant reply to a highly controversial book, *The Myth of God Incarnate*, which is about to be launched by the S.C.M. Press. It's being edited by John Hick. It questions the divinity of Christ. So it hits the headlines S.C.M. have fixed a press conference in the Chapter House of St. Paul's.'

'The Dean's unwise to allow it,' I said. The Dean, Dr. Martin Sullivan, a New Zealander, was a Hodder author and good friend of the firm. 'S.C.M. will make money but the Dean will make trouble.'

Canon Green would edit the reply and write the opening chapter. Others would be written by Bishop Stephen Neill, Bishop Christopher Butler, Brian Hebblethwaite of Queen's College, Cambridge, and Professor John Macquarrie of Oxford. Representing various branches of the church, they would state categorically that most Christians remained confident of the basic truths of the creed.

'What will you call it?' I asked.

'The S.C.M. book will be *The Myth of God Incarnate* so why not *The Truth of God Incarnate*?'

'Michael, I like it. But can you write the book in three weeks if Hodder will manufacture in three weeks? If so, I'll talk to my colleagues.'

'We'll do it,' he said, 'if it will mean publication six weeks from today.'

'I'll have to persuade my colleagues. They'll have to find a printer to co-operate. If they say yes, we'll commission a jacket this morning.'

I explained the situation to Michael Attenborough and Eric Major, sought the goodwill of the chairman, the co-operation of David Dick, our production manager, and the trade and distribution department executives, and talked with the sales directors. In two hours I telephoned Michael.

'You're on,' I said. 'Everybody says, "Let's have a go".' We'll publish a low-price mass market paperback a third of the price of the S.C.M. book. But Michael . . . I've promised not to ask for another miracle for three years!'

As I spoke on the telephone David Dick was finding a printer who could rearrange his schedules to fit in the book. The art department were sketching out a jacket design. Tony Collins, my immediate colleague, was thinking of a press conference. 'If the Dean's loaned St. Paul's to launch the *Myth*,' he said, 'he ought to let us have it to launch the *Truth*.'

'Michael,' I said, 'one question. If the S.C.M. book isn't out how do you know its content?'

He laughed. 'I've got a proof copy,' he said. 'It was sent to a professor here for a review in a theological journal. I asked if I could borrow it. He told me he'd thrown it in the dustbin! Happily, the dustbin hadn't been emptied, so he rummaged round and found it. He brought it over with an apology for the smell.'

On publication the *Myth* received massive press coverage because of the reception for journalists in the Chapter House of St. Paul's. The S.C.M. Press put all their muscle into it. It signalled the start of what a journalist called 'a long, hot and noisy theological summer'.

'Round one,' said the London *Evening Standard*, 'clearly went to the "Jesus was an ordinary chap" school of thought.' The *Catholic Herald* described it as 'the most sensational book of the year, emerging during the quiet season to blazen its message that Christ was not, perhaps, the Son of God.' But the *Financial Times* commented: 'The *Myth* falls apart on a great beam of error'.

Dr. John Robinson, author of *Honest to God*, took his own publisher, S.C.M., to task in a review in *The Times Literary Supplement* for the ill-advised decision to launch it with a press conference. For it hardly merits such publicity. It is more than usually uneven for a symposium. After an encouraging start the layman who has been persuaded to read it is likely to get hopelessly bogged down. What the book lacks is a solid contribution from the systematic or doctrinal theologian as to how Jesus is to be understood positively if he is *not* 'literally' God or a 'literal' incarnation of him.

The Archbishop of York, Dr. Stuart Blanch, said it scarcely did justice to the New Testament, or to subsequent Christian experience. The authors of the New Testament, the Archbishop said, held themselves to be in the presence not just of a special man but of God.

The Reverend Joseph McCullough, in *Books and Bookmen*, marvelled that some books were ever published.

Within this category I would be inclined to number *The Myth of God Incarnate* which, it is obviously hoped, would sell because of the 'shock' effect of its title, especially on the avid media . . . The kind of reinterpretation which the *Myth* proposes is a Christianity without Christ, which so far from enabling modern man to come to the knowledge of faith must considerably increase his doubt and confusion . . . It would seem unlikely in the present situation that many who now halt on the threshold of Christian faith would be attracted across it by churchmen who profess that faith without Christ.

Michael Green rallied his contributors, all busy men, and to my astonishment, and relief, delivered the manuscript of *The Truth of God Incarnate* on schedule: the printers did the typesetting almost overnight, and delivered finished books into the Hodder warehouse within three weeks. It was a first-class team effort, made possible by the goodwill which existed at the printer's and within Hodder.

The Dean of St. Paul's after consultation with his Chapter, gave permission for us to use the historic Chapter House, and on the morning of the press conference he met me at the door. He stayed as Bishop Neill and Canon Green faced the press and photographers.

We made page one of *The Times*. Clifford Longley, the Religious Affairs Correspondent wrote:

> The message is that the belief that Jesus Christ was the son of God is still a tenable proposition for intelligent and reasonable men . . . The five say in their introduction that the gradual abandonment of doctrinal beliefs within the church is analogous to stripping a car; having taken out the engine with the 'Death of God' school of theology, the sceptics are now dismantling the chassis of incarnational belief which held the whole thing together.

*The Times* referred to 'five champions of orthodoxy', a leading evangelical, with Anglo-Catholics and a Roman Catholic reasserting their faith in the ancient dogma of the Incarnation.

*The Times* report alone justified the publication of the book. It told hundreds of thousands of readers that the *Myth* did not represent the view of these responsible Christian leaders and a host like them. From a media viewpoint it had been vital to get a statement out rather than to work leisurely on a polished manuscript.

'*Dustbin hunt aided Jesus "truth team*', was the headline in the *Daily Telegraph*. '*Countering' "Myth" with "Truth"*', said the *Irish Times*. '*That "Myth" is deftly demolished,*' was *The Universe* headline, while *The Guardian* reported, '*Jesus "Myth" book attacked,*' and the *Daily Mail*, '*God fights back*'.

The first printing of the Hodder book was 20,000 copies; within twenty-four hours a reprint was ordered. *The Universe* congratulated authors and publisher:

> The promptness with which it has been produced is in itself reassuring, for if there was ever a time when alertness in stemming the spread of error regarding the fundamentals of the faith was the order of the day, it is now . . . This is the kind of book we need. It makes us aware of the firm foundation of our faith, it is never more

128

than a step away from inspiring us with a deeper attach-
ment to a living faith.

*The Manchester Evening News* made a similar point,
speaking of ordinary believers who are content to go on
living out a faith that they have found to be true and which
is nourished by regular worship, who suddenly read press
reports of learned men and women making out that Jesus
isn't quite what they thought him to be.

They must wonder just a little what is happening to the
spiritual foundation of their lives. It is just as well,
therefore, that an answer to the theological sceptics has
appeared this week . . . Perhaps it is all pin-pointed in
one dramatic demand put to him by a disciple, Philip,
who pleaded: 'Lord, show us the Father'. Jesus told him:
'He who has seen me has seen the Father'. And there you
have it – God in Christ.

S.C.M. Press, with sixty new titles a year, and a total of
500 books in print, covers such a range that it is difficult to
describe. The Reverend John Bowden, its managing director, is an able theologian with an active social conscience,
who doesn't think the term 'religious publishing' has ever
been very useful. 'Books about religion and theology,' he
says, 'cover an enormous range from academic mono-
graphs and textbooks to popular uplift; from books which
try to push human insight into the most difficult of all
subjects as far as it will go, or to express home truths, which
are not likely to be very welcome, to books which are quite
clearly out to exploit a far-fetched or fashionable idea as a
religious bestseller.'

It was an S.C.M. title, *The Adventure of Living*, that
proved so decisive for me, but had the Press, with its
weighty theological backlist, blundered or acted irrespon-
sibly in publishing and trumpeting about the *Myth*, in using
that word in the title with its different theological inter-
pretations? Yes! They were ill-advised in publishing and
erred in endeavouring to work it up into 'the biggest
theological controversy since *Honest to God*'. But publishers are as fallible as authors, editors as vicars, the

S.C.M. Press as Hodder and Stoughton.

The specialist evangelical publishing houses, with their Biblical emphasis, are no exception, and here I should, no doubt, make my own publishing confession. It would take a chapter but I hesitate to publicise the books which, on reflection, I should not have taken.

Reviewers sometimes tell a publisher what these are but the professionals are influenced little by the critics whose conclusions are so diverse. Not so authors. Their creativity can be blocked for months. Yet an editor's choice of reviewer, as much as the content of a book, can determine whether an author basks in glory or puts away his typewriter. There are few notable religious book critics, David Edwards in the *Church Times* being an exception, but a publisher accepts as a benediction the space which editors donate to his wares.

'The true publisher,' says an American commentator on the book trade, 'moves with equal comfort in the world of mind and art and in the world of commerce.' Certainly, one must hold the balance between quality and solvency. I discussed this once with Clayton Carlson, then religious editor of Harper and Row, in New York. 'The dream of having value *and* commercial success,' he said, 'is the dream that keeps us going.' Of all people a religious publisher must look at the quality of his product as well as at the profits. That might mean deliberately turning aside from a potential bestseller. I know how hard that can be.

If we may return to the *Myth*. Forgetting the publishers, were the authors heretics? If so, how should the church deal with them? John Stott raised the issue in *All Souls Magazine*:

The New Testament authors are particularly concerned not so much about false brethren as about false *teachers*, who act like wolves and scatter and destroy Christ's flock. Although the contributors to *The Myth of God Incarnate* are academics, most are also ordained Anglican clergymen who hold a bishop's licence to preach. Is it too much to hope and pray that some bishop sometime will have the courage to withdraw his licence from a presbyter who denies the incarnation?

This would not be an infringement of civil or academic liberty . . . A man may believe, say and write what he pleases in the country and in the university. But *in the church* it is reasonable and right to expect all accredited teachers to teach the faith which the church in its official formularies confesses, and which (incidentally) they themselves have promised to uphold.

# 15

# MAKING MEN WHOLE

I first met Ann on Sunday October, 18th, 1970. On that day I had been to Hamble, near Southampton, to see Chay Blyth off on his round-the-world solo sail. It had been described as 'the impossible voyage'. He had chosen to sail round the world 'the uphill way': in the opposite direction to Francis Chichester, Alex Rose and Robin Knox-Johnston. Robin Denniston had asked me to be his editor and if possible during the journey to contact him at sea by radio telephone.

As the fifty-nine foot boat under sail began its 30,000 mile ocean journey, I slipped a small wooden cross from my study desk into his hand and promised to pray. Once I spoke to him by radio telephone. In 292 days he was back having achieved the impossible.

After his departure I hurried home to Purley to find we had guests. Dr. Ruth Fowke, a friend and author, had brought Dr. Ann Varcoe to tea. They had finished their meal when I arrived. I had about an hour with them but the memory of Ann lingered over the years.

She was a missionary in Thailand with the Overseas Missionary Fellowship, formerly the China Island Mission, founded by Dr. James Hudson Taylor. Her resolve to be her best for God remained with Gwen and myself. When she returned to Thailand, Gwen wrote to her and prayed for her each morning around eight thirty. Of all her missionary friends, Gwen selected Ann for special prayer.

After Gwen's death I learned that Ann had been sent home to England for medical treatment, had made a slow but complete recovery, and was now doing obstetrics and gynaecology at St. Helier Hospital, on the outskirts of South London. She would not be returning to Thailand. We exchanged Christmas cards and I invited her to dinner at the Selsdon Park Hotel. I did not choose well. She found the menu overwhelming. Missionaries had a simpler life-style. We talked easily, as if we had been friends a long time, were stimulated by each other's company, and I dared to hope my loneliness was ending. She was tall and dark with soft blue eyes.

After I returned from Russia, on St. Valentine's Day, I asked her to marry me. She had hardly slept for three nights, having been 'on call', with clinics and operating theatre in the day – the non-stop demands of hospital life. She had come out to eat, determined to stay awake. I did not prolong the meal, but before I left her at the hospital entrance I asked the question which would determine our future.

I can still hardly believe that she said Yes. The lovely life we have together and the home she has created in the last four years convince me it is true. Our wedding service was conducted by the Reverend David Pawson, in the Baptist Church in Guildford.

'We praise you from the bottom of our hearts for the deep sense we have that what we are about to do is your will,' said David in his opening prayer. 'You have enriched Edward's life and Ann's life in so many ways to prepare them for this partnership which now we are going to seal. We want to look back and give you thanks for the way you have led them both, for the experiences both happy and sad, both uplifting and testing which have formed their characters and suited them for each other.'

The service was recorded so that on wedding anniversaries we could re-live the experience, renew the vows and return thanks.

'I get a glimpse of God,' said David in his address, 'of God wanting to make people completely whole. I believe he knew you needed each other for completeness. God looked down from heaven and said, "It is not good that man should dwell alone." God has brought you together as complementary people. God has matched you for a minis-try of making others whole. Together you have had such a varied experience, at home and overseas, of being married, of being single, of looking after people's minds and what they read, of looking after people's bodies and their health, and yet not seeing people as parts but seeing them as whole; people with needs of the body which are affected by the mind.'

'Edward, I've noticed in the books that you've chosen that you've sensed what people's hearts need as well as their minds, and what will reach the emotional as well as the intellectual part of a person. And God has said, "I can put you together to be aware of people's physical condition, mental condition, emotional needs." Together you are going to have a ministry of making other people whole by having experienced together God making you more whole than you were.'

At the conclusion of the service, Ann's Dutch friend, Teo van der Weele, an ex-Thailand missionary, prayed: 'I ask you for a song in their marriage and a song in their home and a lightness of spirit especially when tired people come, heavy laden, who have to find out how much peace and rest you give.'

Before we left the church to sign the wedding register there was this prophecy. 'The Lord gives you this commission to make people whole, by giving them wholesome books to read, by making your home a place of peace, by sharing with those who do not have the privilege of marriage the joy of your family life, by looking forward to the wholeness of Christ when his body is complete in glory.'

We spent our honeymoon in Cornwall, then seven months later Ann took me to Thailand to visit the hospital in Manorom where she had spent her missionary years. Manorom is a market town, population 3,000, in the flat central rice-growing region, beside the Chaophraya river which flows down to Bangkok 120 miles to the south. The hospital, half a mile from the market, is surrounded by paddy fields. When there is severe flooding the ground floor of the hospital may be submerged and the boats come out. It opened in 1956 with eighteen beds. The 100-bed, four-storey hospital I saw was completed in 1969.

We arrived in February. On Saturday, January 14th,

1978, there had been a tragedy. A large van pulled out abruptly and crashed head-on with the hospital mini-bus. Five missionaries with three unborn babies and seven young children were killed. These included two surgeons and their entire families. Five others were injured.

'We've come at the wrong moment?' I suggested.

'No,' said Ann. 'It's the proper time to be here.'

It was. As we went round Ann's surviving friends each told us their story of the terrible day at the isolated hospital, which had no telephone; of the arrival of the injured and the dead, of the doctors and nurses fighting to save the lives of their relatives and colleagues.

'Why did God allow it?' We waited for the question as one by one we met the missionaries. They had crossed the world to spread the news that God is good. They believed he was omnipotent. Could this be his will? In our presence, at least, the question was not voiced. The General Director of the Mission had used the words of Paul to the Philippians in his cable on hearing the news: 'Don't allow questions you can't understand limit the joyous certainties you already know.'

We met Adele and Ulrich Juzi, who had lost one son, Lukas: another son, Joni, was hurt. Long missionary experience had taught them that Christians are not given immunity from sickness or the accidents that others encounter. Not so long before two O.M.F. missionary nurses, Minka and Margaret, had been murdered.

At the gate of the small wooden house, with mosquito netting instead of window-panes, where Ann once lived, we stopped to talk with Adele. She told us of the young Thai who was first at the scene of the accident. His immediate help in organising the transport of the survivors to the hospital probably saved Joni's life. He had been thrown about ten metres and was in a severe state of shock when he arrived at the hospital. He did not know his brother was dead.

'No humans were able to perceive the angels present at the accident scene,' Adele and Ulrich later wrote, 'but we believe they were there, to receive some into eternity and to protect others and save them for more service in their earthly bodies.'

Only one surgeon, Dr. Bryan Parry, survived to deal with the injured. He had lost his wife and two of his three children. Joni, he found, had severe haemorrhage but no internal organs were damaged: in five days he was discharged.

Not so Dr. Julia Brown, Ann's friend from Cardiff. Her hospital treatment would be prolonged. Her survival was a miracle, and Peter Farrington's stitches would avoid disfiguring scars.

The surviving missionaries who were not on duty gave a celebration supper for us that night. They wanted to show their love for Ann and to welcome me. The ladies put on their long cotton dresses and in the fashion of all missionaries brought out their best food, sharing the delicacies which had been preserved for such an event.

I have attended many supper parties. There was the surprise invitation from New York, a cable from Fleming H. Revell Publishers, inviting me to dinner the following Tuesday in Manhattan in honour of Marjorie Holmes whose book, *Two from Galilee*, had made the bestseller charts. With the invitation was an offer to pay my return air fare and hotel expenses. Such is American generosity. Surmising I would never travel so far again for supper, I went.

But that was not comparable with this occasion. We almost wept when Julia Brown was gently wheeled in. Her two arms were in plaster, her left lower leg in plaster and a pin was fixed in her left upper leg to correct a compound fracture. She was accompanied by her mother who had left her husband and home in Cardiff to nurse her. It was a supper with broken limbs and broken hearts and, as when bread was broken at the Last Supper, Christ was there – making us whole.

What a book there is in this place, I told myself. It was an unworthy thought. I was accustomed to them. 'Don't,' a voice whispered. 'This is holy ground. Not yet. Maybe never.'

I was there as a privileged guest not as a publisher. I did not wish to expose the heartache, the tears, those raw wounds. I had become part of the experience for those twenty-four hours and I could not capitalise on it. If it had

136

happened in an earlier year my own dear Ann might have been in that mini-bus.

In Ecclesiastes we read to everything there is a season and a time to every purpose under heaven. 'A time to be born, and a time to die; a time to plant, and a time to pluck up that which is planted . . . a time to keep silence, and a time to speak.' That uncannily perceptive commentator, Matthew Henry, tells us there is a time when it becomes us, and is our wisdom and duty, to keep silence, when we are in danger of speaking amiss; but there is also a time to speak for the glory of God and the edification of others, when silence would be the betraying of a righteous cause. 'It is a great part of Christian prudence,' he said, 'to know when to speak and when to hold our peace.'

There are books, especially in the field of personal experience, many originating in America, where there is a danger of publishing out of time, or amiss, where wisdom and duty demand rejection. Give them what they want? Not always! To do that, in the words of Clayton Carlson, would be to accept 'a more respectable, socially acceptable variation of the self-same dynamics that go on in the porno publishing business. Surely they give the people what they want.'

To paraphrase Matthew Henry: 'It is a great part of Christian publishing to know when to publish and when to hold off.'

# 16

# GOD'S BOOK

'We're weary with new translations of the Bible. Don'
inflict another on us.'

'Young people will be more confused if Hodder pub
lishes the *New International Version*.'

'Another Bible. Is it necessary?' Discouraging comment
in 1975 from clergy, booksellers, friends. If the reaction
had been fed into a computer as part of market research
Hodder would have been advised not to launch the N.I.V

Against these seemingly reasonable statements we ha
to weigh the claim that the N.I.V. was the first trul
international translation, with more than one hundre
scholars from the major English-speaking countries of th
world – America, Canada, England, Australia, New Zea
land; that twenty years of research and painstaking analysi
had made possible the most accurate, readable and dig
nified version, suitable for personal devotions and study a
well as public reading, memorising and evangelism.

Each book of the Bible has been assigned to a sma
group of scholars for the first or 'team' translation. Nex
Intermediate Editorial Committees reviewed the tear
translations with constant reference to the Hebrew, Ara
maic, and Greek texts. These then went to the Genera
Editorial Committees – at many sessions a stylist joine
these. Finally, the translations, now in their third draf
were reviewed and revised once more, this time by th
Committee on Bible Translation. Thus the entire Bible
book by book, was translated and revised again and again

Working at a maximum rate of five verses an hour, the

watched for faithfulness to the original text and quality of English style. Although the scholars, from many denominations, were committed to the full authority and complete trustworthiness of the Bible as God's Word, there was no striving for an 'evangelical translation' but rather for one through which the Bible itself will speak as it wants to speak'.

My task was to advise Hodder and Stoughton whether to take on the awesome responsibility of launching the N.I.V. this side of the Atlantic. The more I sought advice the more discouraged I became.

'Since the war,' I was reminded, 'we've had the publication of the Revised Standard Version, J. B. Phillips' New Testament, the New English Bible, the Living Bible, the Jerusalem Bible and the Good News Bible. Isn't that sufficient? And, thank God, we still have the Authorised Version.'

I called a meeting in the Hodder boardroom of Christian leaders, seeking their views and hoping to persuade them that the search for greater faithfulness to the original is never wholly finished. I sought a mandate to publish. Professor Donald Wiseman, of London University, one of the translators, chaired the meeting. The response was mainly negative.

There were two or three months in which to make the decision. If we published and it proved a mistake the loss might easily exceed £100,000. If we failed to publish and it subsequently proved itself, the firm would have missed a unique opportunity. I browsed through *Word and World*, the story of the English Bible, which Hodder had published for Donald Coggan when he was Archbishop of York. I found the lot of Bible translators, printers and publishers was not a happy one.

One of the early translations of fragments of Scripture into the native tongue was by the Venerable Bede (673–'35). He was translating the Gospel of John. Sitting on the floor of his cell he died as he completed the last sentence.

John Purcey, who was closely associated with the Wycliffe Bible, was imprisoned. Likewise his companion Nicholas Hereford who, Lord Coggan tells us, was persecuted both in Rome, where he made an appeal to the Pope, and in England, where he was imprisoned. Wycliffe closed his life in peace but after his death his body and bones were exhumed and publicly burnt 'and his ashes disposed of that no trace of him shall be seen again'.

William Tyndale's translation, begun in 1525, filtered into Britain in bales of cotton and by other secret means. The Archbishop of Canterbury bought up copies and burned them at St. Paul's Cross. Tyndale was martyred in 1536. His last prayer was, 'Lord, open the King of England's eyes.'

In the seventeenth century a London printer was sent to prison for publishing the Adulterer's Bible. The commandment 'Thou shalt not commit adultery' omitted the 'not'.

Hodder had sponsored two modern versions this century – without mishap. First, the Moffatt Bible in 1924, of which Lord Coggan writes: 'The credit of being a pioneer in this field rests with this great Scotsman . . . The production was a landmark in the story of modern biblical translation. Dr. Moffatt was a Biblican theologian and church historian of international reputation.'

In 1967 I met Dr. Kenneth Taylor who was then nearing completion of his paraphrase The Living Bible, which was to sell some twenty-five million copies around the world. He and his British director, the Reverend Dr. Jack Hywel Davies, gave permission for Hodder to launch this in the British Commonwealth jointly with Coverdale (now Kingsway Publications).

This paraphrase was born at the dinner table when Dr Taylor was reading to eight of his children from the Epistle to Timothy in the Authorised Version. They found it hard to understand. He pondered the problem on his way to Moody Press where he was an editor, then the idea came 'Why not write tonight's Bible reading in words the children will understand?' He arrived home that night with a chapter ready for them and so began one of the most important jobs ever to be tackled on a morning and evening commuter train. When he had worked right through the Epistles he sent copies to New Testament scholars for comment. More work followed. In 1961 he published

*Living Letters*, then tackled the minor prophets. In 1970 he handed me the text of the complete Living Bible. It had taken fourteen years.

Within seven months one and a half million copies were sold.

'Ken,' I asked, 'what are you going to do with all the royalties?' When he told me they were going into a charity called the Living Bible Foundation my admiration for him soared higher. I made a confession. 'I think God might have trusted me with the paraphrasing, if I'd had the ability, but I'm not sure he could have trusted me to give all those royalties away.'

There is no perfect translation. Complete objectivity is not attainable. The New York International Bible Society, which sponsored the N.I.V. said, 'No translator, regardless of his view of the Bible, works in a theological and philosophical vacuum. Computers may be wholly objective; scholars are not. Presuppositions and convictions cannot be divorced from their work, but for a scholar to hold to the authority and infallibility of the Bible means that he must in all things respect the integrity of the Bible . . . that means an overruling concern to be faithful to the text of Scripture.'

The finance and the commitment needed to launch a Bible is frightening. This is because of the huge printings demanded to achieve competitive prices.

At Church House, the administrative hub of the Anglican Church, in the Baptist Union, in the Methodist Conference, in the Church of Scotland, in the religious department of the B.B.C., there was not a glimmer of interest. I posted a copy of the N.I.V. New Testament to John Stott begging for a commendation: he was too busy, about to go abroad. All Souls had recently purchased the R.S.V. for its pews. I talked with Nigel Sylvester, the General Secretary of Scripture Union, with its deep concern for daily Bible reading, but he was hesitant. I called on the Bible Society in London but their representative only wished to share their plans for the *Good News Bible*.

The booksellers, who benefit substantially from new translations, prophesied doom. Not one bookseller advised positively.

141

Every indicator suggested Hodder should not sign the contract. Except one. The Gideons who place Bibles in schools, hotels, hospitals, prisons and similar institutions believed their executive might support it. They were still distributing the Authorised Version, having found other translations unacceptable. They would not, however, be able to make a decision until their executive had read the complete text – in three years' time.

I shared my findings with Professor Wiseman. 'I promise you,' he said, 'that five years after publication the N.I.V will have a permanent place in the life of many churches. I will take time to establish itself. But don't miss the opportunity.'

'It's a long time to have stock in the warehouse,' I said 'To make sense of it we'll need large sales in the first months.' We finished our sandwiches in his office and walked down Charing Cross Road, past the famous book shops.

'God,' I prayed. 'This is your book. If there's a place for it give me, give Hodder, the courage to make a commitment that will not waver.'

I like to make my own decisions, but now I wanted to share the responsibility. It was too big for me. I talked frankly with Philip and Michael Attenborough and with Eric Major, who had known Bible publishing in his days a Collins. I told them of the lukewarm response I had received. I shared my belief that there must be a market for a translation where the overruling concern had been faithfulness to the text of Scripture. I explained how the Gideons had been attracted by this aspect. They saw my faith – and my fear.

'Let's publish,' said the chairman. 'Agreed,' said Michael and Eric. From that day the firm was fully committed, whatever the cost, whatever the outcome.

My problems were not over.

The first concerned anglicisation: taking out the Americanisms, substituting English spelling, and pounds for dollars.

Professor Wiseman with a small team of helpers was responsible for recommending the changes necessary for this country. The problem, from the Hodder viewpoint

142

was that the recommendations would be subject to American approval! Seen from the States this was reasonable. Scholars who had spent years determining every word should be given an opportunity of seeing any changes made in London before printing commenced. From my office I guessed it would lead to constant frustration and delay. It did.

I imagine it took the Apostle Paul less time to write an epistle than it did for us to come to a common mind on words which had different shades of meaning on different sides of the Atlantic. Sometimes Americans were happy with one word in all circumstances, whereas the English reader was more precise, and would require more subtle variation. 'Grain' and/or 'corn', 'round and/or around', 'so' and/or 'so that' – these were the dizzying details of many months' correspondence.

'Don't publish until there's agreement,' was the message from the States. That was impossible if the British publication was to be within a few months of the American. Ideally, they should have been published simultaneously, a fact the scholars did not appreciate.

Although Hodder had exclusive rights in the British traditional markets there was no way to keep out unanglicised American editions if there was too wide a gap between the American and the British launch. This meant smaller print runs in London and subsequently higher prices.

To drum up support overseas I went to Australia and New Zealand in Autumn 1977 to speak at the Christian Booksellers' Annual Conferences. In Australia, Hodder's managing director, Edward Coffey, one of the world's great salesmen, and his religious book specialist, Helen Harrison, at least his equal in selling Christian books, fixed a press conference for me in Sydney. The result of Helen's initiative astonished me. Months later I was still receiving press cuttings from around the world. An Indian daily newspaper reported that I likened the various translations of the Bible, with their different language levels, to clothing apparel. The Living Bible was the Scriptures in pyjamas; the Good News Bible was in sports clothes; the Revised Standard Version was in dinner-dress with bow-tie; the

143

New International Version was in office suit; and the
Authorised Version was in tails and top hat. As we have a
wardrobe of clothes so there was need for a variety of
translations.

In New Zealand, Ron Coombes, the managing director
arranged television, radio and press interviews, while en
during almost unbearable pain from a back problem which
put him into hospital. In neither Australia nor New Zea
land did the salesman ask if the N.I.V. would succeed: the
Hodder commitment created the initative to give it every
opportunity of doing so. The booksellers assured us of
support.

How many should we print? Michael Attenborough
with David Dick and Harry Maple in the production de
partment, supervised the costing. A minimum first printing
of 100,000 copies, with a book of one thousand two hun
dred pages, would give a competitive retail price. Here
made a mistake. The translators, Dr. Y. R. Kindberg, the
President of the New York International Bible Society
told me, had not wasted words. This meant that if other
Bibles made an average of twelve hundred pages the N.I.V.
should not be longer, I told myself. Indeed the N.I.V. ha
an elegance and a leanness of style. But I failed to allow in
my calculations that the beautiful layout would spread the
book. The N.I.V. poetry is printed as poetry; the genealo
gies and the lists of those returning from captivity are
printed so as to show what they are and assist ready
reference to them. In the New Testament the salutations to
the Epistles are printed to show their distinctive form.
arrived back from New Zealand to learn the N.I.V. wa
making two hundred more pages than we had allowed for
Our estimated profit took a plunge.

We had four months in which to proof-read the complete
Bible. It was impossible. It had to be done. Five people
some staff some outsiders, would read the complete proofs
including Professor Wiseman who would be responsible for
anglicisation checks.

Only those who have attempted such an exercise can
know the cost to the individual, the enormity of the under
taking. Clifford Longley, Religious Affairs Corresponden
of *The Times*, failed to cheer me by warning that 'not' can

easily become 'now'. I shuddered, thinking of the ten commandments.

Rosemary Croucher collated the corrections as the proofs came from the five readers. Each had numerous queries. Should this word be spelt with an 's' or a 'z'? Was the style in the footnotes in Genesis consistent with those in Isaiah?

Tony Collins came to my home one weekend. We had decided to read the proofs aloud to each other. After a few hours we were hoarse. It had to be done alone. David Dick master-minded feeding the corrections to the printer. Later, Rob Warner, with a First Class honours degree and masters in English, joined us to compare line by line, word by word, the English and American setting, to list for the Americans every anglicisation. His powers of concentration and grasp of both language and Scripture lifted some of the burden from Tony and myself, who were visibly flagging.

In the production department I overheard the comment that they were glad most of our authors wrote shorter books. When we reached the book of Revelations we had made four thousand corrections, mostly tiny but essential in a Bible where perfection in layout and language is sought. Long-distance runners in sight of the finishing post don't relax. Happily, nor did we. Revelation, the final book, has twenty-two chapters. In chapter nineteen, verse fifteen, which should have read: 'If anyone's name was not written in the book of life, he was thrown into the lake of fire,' there was a misprint. The word 'not' was missing.

'Thank God, we found it,' we said, knowing Hazell, Watson and Viney were already printing the first sheets. If the mistake had been discovered after the Bibles were printed not one could have been sold.

Our pre-publication order had jumped to 180,000, as the representatives conveyed their enthusiasm to the booksellers. Richard Barnes, our religious sales specialist in Britain, was sure he would never market a better product. Better than most, he was able to assess the quality of the translation. Our publicity department succeeded in putting its publication into the B.B.C. television news programmes. That week a service of thanksgiving for the N.I.V. was held in St. Martin in the Fields, Trafalgar Square, with representatives of the Gideons and the Bible Society participating, and Dr. W. J. Martin and Professor Sir Norman Anderson giving the addresses.

'Our first printing should have been 250,000,' Jim McEwen, our tireless sales director, told me. 'You should have had more faith!'

'We urgently need 50,000 for Australia,' said Warwick Bailey, the export sales director. 'We've got to get them there quickly.'

When I saw the reviews I agreed. Anthony Burgess in *The Observer* described it as 'very readable . . . This is the Word of God as seen through glass clearly . . . beautifully presented and superbly printed'; while in the *Daily Express* Peter Grosvenor wrote: 'What bowls you over as you read the *New International Version* is quite how much of the old Bible you misunderstood.' Dr. Henry Chadwick, the Dean of Christ Church, wrote in the *Daily Telegraph*: 'The translators have had considerable success.'

In 1980 Hodder published *The Alternative Service Book 1980*, to be used in thousands of parish churches in Britain. That was described as the greatest publishing event in the Church of England for 300 years, but even that did not measure up, in my experience, to launching a new translation of God's Book.

Today, the Gideons in Britain use it widely, voting it the best translation since the Authorised Version. John Stott sent a recommendation in time for publication:

What does one hope for in translators of the Bible? First, a humble reverence before the sacred text; second, scholarly familiarity with the theology, background and language of the Bible; and thirdly, cultural sensitivity into the search for a 'dynamic equivalent' which is both faithful and appropriate. The N.I.V. seems to me to reflect an outstanding combination of these three qualities, and I warmly commend it.

When the translators had completed their task they recognised with gratitude the help of Almighty God in doing their work. Most of all they had been humbled by the sheer

146

greatness of the Bible itself. It was exactly how Tony Collins, Rob Warner and I felt.

Not every Bible has been published without unfortunate misprints. Here are three:

*The Sin on Bible* (1716). John 5: 14 reads: 'sin on more', instead of 'sin no more'.

*The Fool Bible* (printed in the reign of Charles I). Psalm 14 reads: 'The fool hath said in his heart there is a God.' The printers were fined £3,000 for substituting 'a' for 'no'.

*The Unrighteous Bible* (1653). 1 Corinthians 6:9 reads: 'Know ye not that the unrighteous shall inherit [for shall not inherit] the Kingdom of God.'

Thousands of Christians lived before the days of printed books. As our author, Dr. J. I. Packer, pointed out in *God Has Spoken* it is not absolutely necessary that one must read and study the Biblical text but he adds: 'One who fails to read the Bible is at an enormous disadvantage. Rightly are Bible-reading and Bible-based meditation seen as prime means of grace. Not only is Scripture the fountain-head for knowledge of God, Christ and salvation, but it presents this knowledge in an incomparably vivid, powerful and evocative way.'

Whatever the translation we must not neglect the reading of this book.

# 17

# I BELIEVE

Rummaging through a secondhand bookstall in a village hall one Saturday afternoon I found and purchased for a few pence a volume which was to inspire the creation of a new series. *This I Believe*, by Edward R. Murrow, was published some twenty-five years ago. It contains the personal philosophies of one hundred thoughtful men and women, fifty British and fifty American, of many faiths and background. For Ed Murrow, a famous radio commentator, what men believe became of great importance to him when he discovered that a friend of his had been killed, not because of what he had done, but because he insisted upon retaining and agitating for his beliefs. He saw the value of brief statements by people who had attempted to define what they believe and why.

I read that the beliefs of men and women changed importantly over the years. Very positive beliefs of young people changed through experience. This was considered natural and good. The only wrong was in not letting your beliefs grow as you grow.

What did these one hundred contributors believe? They were businessmen, lawyers, physicians, writers, lecturers, sportsmen, actors. Few had a Biblical faith. Most had no church connection, although often faith in a Supreme Being did form part of their creed. I underlined some of the common beliefs.

Those who were not able to believe the Christian faith normally endeavoured to live by its principles. They believed in the sanctity of the individual; in Schweitzer's 'reverence for life'; that life is worth-while; in tolerance, in truth, in courage, in progress, in the family; that love is more fertile than hate, that good is stronger than evil. Some believed in life after death, others in a progress towards a heaven on earth. Most had hope.

Viscountess Astor, who achieved fame by becoming the first woman member of Parliament, believed in God, the Bible and that 'the English thinking people are the hope of the world today'. A minority believed that every individual is a living soul, whose destiny did not begin and whose significance does not end with life on this planet.

*This I Believe* started as a radio programme. It reached 39,000,000 people in the United States alone. It became the most listened-to radio programme in the world. It was broadcast 900 times a week on 150 overseas stations. Some eighty-five newspapers carried the 'I Believe' feature. The book I had bought had been published by popular demand.

*I Believe*: what a magnificent title, was my first thought, for a Christian book outlining the faith. No. Why not a series? Twelve or fifteen books, possibly based on the Creed. Find a trusted editor. I thought of Canon Michael Green, then still principal of St. John's who combined evangelistic thrust with academic distinction and had a contagious enthusiasm which would inspire the writers.

I went to Nottingham and in his home in the college grounds we talked until midnight. The next morning, as we walked from his car to the railway platform, he agreed to edit twelve to fifteen volumes, including one he would write himself on the Holy Spirit.

Because Michael was the editor, Eerdmans, the American publisher, immediately made a commitment to publish the complete series, before a volume was written. Arrangements for German and Swedish translations followed. So far volumes on the following topics have been written: *I Believe in the Resurrection of Jesus*; in *Revelation*; in *Evangelism*; in the *Church*; in the *Historical Jesus*; in *Man*; in the *Second Coming of Jesus*; in the *Great Commissions*; in the *Holy Spirit*; in *Preaching*; in the *Creator*; in *Church Growth*; and in *Satan's Downfall*. This last title caused some headache. No one wanted to publish a book called *I Believe in Satan*. The solution was to add the word '*Downfall*'.

Ed Murrow's book succeeded because it came from a

man's life, that which constitutes him. Michael Green shared the view that this series should combine scholarship and experience, and he set about commissioning an international, trans-cultural, and interconfessional team. As he put it, the books should come from writers, 'with one foot firmly placed in the Bible, and the other foot firmly placed in the contemporary scene'.

This meant, for example, that for a volume on evangelism we would not contract a professor or lecturer but an evangelist. The obvious choice was the Reverend David Watson of York. Of David, Michael Green wrote:

> After a baptism of fire in the dockland parish of Gillingham where he served a distinguished curacy followed by a spell in as different a milieu as you could imagine, among the undergraduates at Cambridge, he went to York and was entrusted with overseeing the funeral rites, so to speak, of an inner city church that was about to close through disuse. Beginning with a tiny handful, he saw the power of the gospel change the lives of countless ordinary citizens of York. His church was soon packed; it was linked up to other halls by closed circuit T.V., and before long he was given charge of a much larger church (also on the verge of closure) right opposite York Minster. It is now thronged with people.

David Watson was well equipped to write about evangelism through his public preaching and personal conversations, in universities throughout the world, in city-wide campaigns and in schools. His ministry was alive with the freshness and power of the Holy Spirit. As an evangelist he had heard continual complaints: 'The church is suffocated with words and starved of experience'; 'The world is satiated with dogmas, but people are hungry for life'; 'Words, words, words – I'm sick of words . . . Show me.' In preparation for a town mission he was reminded by the committee that most people now had become 'word-resistant'. He believed that, from New Testament days to the twentieth century, unless there is a demonstration of the power of the Spirit, the proclamation of the gospel will be in vain. It will not be true evangelism.

150

One of the remarkable evangelistic missions he had the privilege of leading illustrates this truth. He had been asked to 'proclaim the good news of Jesus Christ' both formally and informally, through services, house-meetings, youth fellowship and so forth. However the context of this proclamation of words had been very rich indeed. He writes:

In the two churches involved there had been a gracious and powerful move of the Spirit of God. This had led to much prayer, an increasing experience of the hitherto unknown gifts of the Spirit (such as prophecy, healing, tongues with interpretation), small fellowship groups meeting regularly, a healthy involvement in the community, and, above all, a warm, loving, welcoming, caring fellowship of God's people – an effective body of Christ. During the long weekend of that mission the spiritual harvest was quite remarkable: approximately a hundred men and women professed faith in Christ on one day alone, and I understand that not only was there a hundred per cent turn-out for the follow-up meeting a few days afterwards, but God's work in those churches has gone on from strength to strength.

Fleet Street's caricatures of the clergy can be provocative. An article in the *Weekend Telegraph* said:

The Anglican priests of England, a motley band of underpaid and generally frustrated men, provide some of the most poignant casualties of the twentieth century. They suffer nervous breakdowns through lack of money, waste hours trudging the countryside, peddling faith to the sceptical, and reap untold depressions by preaching in ill-repaired churches to diminishing and elderly congregations.

But David Watson, and indeed the vicars I know best, are far removed from this scornful picture.

Since his book on evangelism and a further volume, *I Believe in the Church*, have been published the evangelist has been discovered by Fleet Street. Peregrine Worsthorne, a senior journalist on the *Sunday Telegraph*, wrote

151

a two-column article, probably read by two million readers, after hearing David preach. He wrote:

> If any political figure was able to pack the Albert Hall on three nights running, mostly with young people, the supposition would be that he was someone of significance, certainly a household name . . . Yet this is what a previously unknown Anglican clergyman did do last week . . . What made him extraordinary was his naturalness: his gift for talking about God as if he did not feel the need to put on a special ecclesiastical voice: nor to associate God with fashionable good causes.

Dorothy Sayers once wrote: 'There are those who would worship the Father, the Son and the Virgin Mary; those who believe in the Father, the Son and the Holy Scriptures; those who found their faith on the Father, the Son and the Church, and there are even those who seem to derive their spiritual power from the Father, the Son and the minister!' David Watson commented: 'The Pentecostal explosion has largely been a reaction to this, with a fresh recognition of the Third Person of the Trinity.'

Michael Green talked with me about a volume entitled *I Believe in God*. We decided not to proceed with the idea. This was because it would be difficult to find a better book than *Knowing God* by Dr. J. I. Packer. That would have fitted admirably into the series but it was written too soon.

*Knowing God* is a book which grew slowly. It started, in the author's words, as 'a string of beads', a series of small studies in a magazine. In 1969 Dr. Packer showed us these articles and asked if they might make the basis of a book. Although they were conceived as separate contributions he planned to present them together to coalesce into a single message about God and our living.

Two or three years later we received the finalised manuscript. It has now sold hundreds of thousands of copies. It is one man declaring his belief in God.

The author's conviction is that ignorance of God – ignorance both of his ways and of the practice of communion with him – lies at the root of much of the church's weakness. Some deny God; for others he has become remote

Men have become pygmy Christians by reducing their view of God to pygmy proportions.

He points out that we are in danger of falling victims to one of two trends. One is to emphasise the importance of man and diminish the importance of God. The second is to be confused by fashionable scepticism. To doubt God is to be 'with it'.

*Knowing God* attempts to bring us to the point where we both can and must get our priorities straight. Dr. Packer writes:

> From current Christian publications you might think that the most vital issue for any real or would-be Christian in the world today is church union, or social witness, or dialogue with other Christians and other faiths, or refuting this or that ism, or developing a Christian philosophy and culture. But our line of study makes the present-day concentration on these things look like a gigantic conspiracy of misdirection. Of course, it is not that; the issues themselves are real and must be dealt with in their place. But it is tragic that, in paying attention to them, so many in our day seem to have been distracted from what was, and is, and always will be the true priority for every human being – that is, learning to know God in Christ.

David Watson was pleading for a fresh recognition of the Holy Spirit, while, in *I Believe in the Historical Jesus*, Dr. I. Howard Marshall pleaded for a rediscovery of Jesus. The author was not only a distinguished lecturer in the University of Aberdeen but had himself, through the Gospels, been brought face to face with the Biblical Jesus. When his manuscript arrived I turned to the last page, as I invariably do, and in the last paragraph I read:

> I believe in the historical Jesus. I believe that historical study confirms that he lived and ministered and taught in a way that is substantially reproduced in the Gospels. I believe that this Jesus gave his life as a ransom for sinful mankind, and that he rose from the dead and is the living Lord. And in view of these facts I trust in him and commit my life to him.

In a church I was honoured by being introduced as the Mr. I. Believe Publisher. I did not deserve the title but I liked it. My call had been to publish for those who had found a faith, who had accepted the Lordship of Christ, who wished to share their discovery with the world. It meant more to me than being described as Mr. Successful Publisher.

But what do I believe? After publishing some 500 Christian books, and examining thousands of unpublished manuscripts, am I confused, bewildered, learning to dodge the fundamental questions?

For me, as for Peter, a confession of faith would start with: 'Thou art the Christ, the son of the living God.' Jesus is God. That is the basis, the focal point of my belief, and nothing which I have read has been able to shatter that.

He is not only God. He is Saviour. My Saviour. I have sought and experienced the forgiveness of the Lord Jesus.

I believe he is Lord. Not a remote figure. Not a legendary figure. Not a memory from an experience in St. Paul's Cathedral. But a presence closer than this paper on which I write, more real than yesterday, more certain than tomorrow.

I have grown in my publishing years less conscious of the 'whats' that divide and more conscious of the 'Whom' that unites. Having persuaded Canon Max Warren to write his autobiography, *Crowded Canvas*, I copied from it these words: 'The wholeness of the Christian experience in this life can be, for any of us, only partial. God made us so different that he must desire that we should seek wholeness in different ways.' I no longer limit God by my own experience of him. I am at home with the people of God whatever their denomination.

Because I was his publisher I was a privileged guest at the enthronement of Donald Coggan as Archbishop of Canterbury. What pageantry! Seated among the guests in Canterbury Cathedral, waiting for the processions to start, listening to the great organ, I did not feel I belonged.

The processions entered by the West Door: the Lord Chancellor, the Speaker of the House of Commons, the Prime Minister; then the deans and provosts and bishops; the archbishops from overseas; the Prince of Wales, Princess Margaret and other members of the Royal Family.

The Archbishop was greeted with a fanfare of trumpets and the choir sang, 'I was glad when they said unto me: we will go into the house of the Lord'. When the Archbishop reached his place and the anthem ended, there were greetings from other Christian communions, prayer, and then the enthronement in the chair of St. Augustine.

From his throne the Archbishop addressed his people. For a few minutes he took us back to the third century, quoting St. Cyprian writing to a man called Donatus:

> This seems a cheerful world, Donatus, when I view it from this fair garden, under the shadow of these vines. But if I climbed some great mountain and looked out over the wide lands, you know very well what I would see. Brigands on the high road, pirates on the seas, in the amphitheatres men murdered to please the applauding crowds, under all roofs misery and selfishness. It is really a bad world, Donatus, an incredibly bad world. Yet in the midst of it I have found a quiet and holy people. They have discovered a joy which is a thousand times better than any pleasure of this sinful life. They are despised and persecuted, but they care not. They have overcome the world. These people, Donatus, are the Christians . . . and I am one of them.

I am one of them. Not a dean nor a bishop, not a politician nor a Lord Mayor, not a moderator or even an archdeacon but one of those who have discovered a joy which is a thousand times better than anything this life can offer. As I listened to the Archbishop I knew where I belonged. With St. Cyprian and Lord Coggan I can say, 'And I am one of them.'

155

# 18

# STEPPING OUT

This book had an obvious starting point: my reading of *The Adventure of Living* by Paul Tournier on the train journey to London, the stepping out to begin a new personal adventure. Since then I had discovered the reality of Tournier's words that God 'brings one adventure to an end only to open another to us . . . With him we must be ready for anything.'

The closing point is equally apparent. On July 31st, 1980, I left Hodder and Stoughton. The possibility had been with me since the publication of the N.I.V. Bible but I wished to complete the negotiations for the *Alternative Service Book, 1980*, and see it safely with the printer. In May, on the dawn of my fiftieth birthday I wrote:

I have completed fourteen years with Hodder and have a normal expectation of a further fifteen years with the firm which has played such a providential part in my life. Hodder Christian books have been my twenty-four hours-a-day concern, and the satisfaction has been great, but I now have the conviction, persistent for the last few weeks, that the time has come to step out into the unknown. I am glad it is unknown. If it were known it would be unlikely to compare with what I have now.

It will mean saying goodbye to the opportunities and the freedom which the company has given me, to the privileges that go with being an executive of an international company, the companionship of the director's dining-room. 'For what?' my friends will ask. 'I don' know,' I will reply, 'but something to do with books: writing, publishing, marketing.'

Today I have said goodbye to Charles Colson, who has been in London for the launching of his book *Life Sentence*. I copied out some words which he quoted from John Haggai:

*Attempt something so impossible that unless God is in it, it is doomed to failure.*

I have talked it over with Ann. She's marvellous. 'Will we have to move house?' she asked. 'Leave my alpines?' Her alpine collection is a source of constant joy. For her birthday we went to an alpine specialist to select some rare varieties.

On May 13th, as beautiful a day as I can recall, we walked around a Sussex village green, breathing in the spring, voicing our thoughts and our expectations of God's goodness. There was blossom everywhere and the rhododendron buds in the cottage gardens shyly showed their colours. We were full of happiness.

The next day, with Ann's blessing, I sent a letter of resignation to Philip Attenborough, who was not only my chairman but a friend and constant ally in the development of the religious list. He summoned me to his office.

'Why? Why?' he asked with genuine concern for my welfare. 'The next fifteen years could be the best. You've a great religious list. Stay and enjoy it.'

He accepted my resignation only after I had talked with his brother, Michael, and with Eric Major. Graciously, he then wrote:

I can recognise, as can Michael and Eric, that you have a design (maybe even a vision!) for your future . . . When the time comes, we shall all wish you and Ann every possible success and happiness whatever you and your future together may have in store. Your principal colleagues, of whom I am privileged to have been one, will miss you enormously . . .

That night Ann and I went to dinner in a restaurant within sight of the South Downs, celebrating a new freedom 'to listen for the wind'.

Ann gave me a slip of paper. She had copied out some words of Dr. Stanley Browne, the eminent leprosy specialist: 'If we only have a vision, we are dreamers; if we merely work we are drudges. We need vision and work, hard work and clear vision.'

The elation at the beginning of a new adventure might have been threatened by the disapproval of friends. A caring author, on behalf of himself and another writer, asked if I was really certain, if the die was cast irrevocably. 'We are both very uneasy . . . We would beg you to think again,' he wrote.

I could not share my future plans. At that time there were none. 'Something worthwhile,' sounded lame. I might have quoted Tournier: 'It is only when we give up the idea we *must* be clear, and let ourselves be led by God blindly, if I may put it so, rather than demanding that he show us clearly at each step what our road is, that we shall get out of difficulty.'

Saying goodbye to the firm, to my colleagues, was painful. It still is. It was not easy loosening those deeply-rooted ties and my new freedom was coloured with genuine sense of loss. Between us we had marketed more than twelve million Christian books.

I had not said goodbye to the books. I live with them in the sitting-room, in the dining-room, in the study. They are books which have changed me. I learned to publish only what fired my own mind and heart. If a book on prayer did not make me pray, if a book on hungry people did not make me give, if a volume on the Holy Spirit did not make me seek his blessing, I turned aside. I was a heart more than a head publisher. Maybe the balance should be changed now. That is a matter for my successors. I thank God for them. Long ago the firm learned to trust its Christian publishing to men and women who believe. Because of this the future is bright. The programme will expand and prosper. Life-changing books will continue to be launched. To authors, editors, and booksellers, I give the words of Thomas à Kempis:

> If he shall not lose his reward who gives a cup of cold water to his thirsty neighbour, what will not be the reward of those who by putting good books into the hands of those neighbours, open to them the fountains of eternal life.

*Edward England is today a publishing consultant and a literary agent limiting himself to fifty Christian authors. In 1981 he became the publisher of* Renewal *magazine.*